SHIPWRECKS
and
SEA MONSTERS
of California's Central Coast

Randall A. Reinstedt

maps and sketches by
Antone A. Hrusa

If bookstores in your area do not carry *SHIPWRECKS AND SEA MONSTERS of California's Central Coast*, copies may be obtained by writing to...

GHOST TOWN PUBLICATIONS

P.O. Drawer 5998
Carmel, Ca. 93921

Other books by Randall A. Reinstedt, offered by Ghost Town Publications, are:

GHOSTS, BANDITS AND LEGENDS of Old Monterey
MONTEREY'S MOTHER LODE
TALES, TREASURES AND PIRATES of Old Monterey
GHOSTLY TALES AND MYSTERIOUS HAPPENINGS of Old Monterey
WHERE HAVE ALL THE SARDINES GONE?
INCREDIBLE GHOSTS of Old Monterey's HOTEL DEL MONTE
INCREDIBLE GHOSTS of the BIG SUR COAST
GHOST NOTES

Eighth Printing

Manufactured in the United States of America

Library of Congress Catalog Card Number 76-350548
ISBN 0-933818-02-5

TABLE OF CONTENTS

INTRODUCTION

In looking at a map of California one can readily see that the historic bay of Monterey lies approximately half-way between her northerly and southerly neighbors of Oregon and Mexico. In taking a closer look at this rugged stretch of central California coast, we find that Monterey's rounded bay also lies approximately half-way between Pescadero Point (to the north) and Pfeiffer Point (to the south). It is these waters and the treacherous coastline in between that this book is about.

Dating from the early years of California's colorful history, to and including maritime tragedies of comparatively recent times, ships of all shapes and sizes have found a watery grave along this stretch of California coast. But, as odd as it sometimes seems, it isn't only shipwrecks that cause heads to shake and old-timers to be sought out for a "one more time" recounting of a favorite sea saga. As often as not, the tales requested from these grizzled sea veterans are about the sightings of strange and unidentified sea creatures that have been observed along the central California coast.

Unlike shipwrecks, which dot the coastline at frequent intervals, the sightings of sea beasts have, for the most part, been limited to Monterey Bay and its immediate environs. Also, unlike the shipwrecks, the great majority of sea monster sagas are from the mid-1900's, and do not date back to the mid-1800's as does the history of shipwrecks.

Other than the text, which brings to light numerous intriguing and little-known facts, "Shipwrecks and Sea Monsters of California's Central Coast" boasts the most complete collection of central California shipwreck and sea monster photos that have ever been assembled. Found in collections from throughout the state, the photographs vividly bring to life the events that made maritime history along the California coast. With sea monsters being somewhat camera shy, it is only natural that the great majority of the illustrations are of ships that came to grief along this rugged stretch of coast. A few of these vessels, as the text will bear out, were only stranded for relatively short periods of time. . . , surviving to once again "tempt fate" as they plied the fog-plagued waters of the Pacific. But the majority of the ships that found their way to the unfriendly shore remained there forever. . . , their once sleek hulls pierced by the jagged rocks or caught in the vise-like grip of the coastal sand. Many of these rusting and rotting hulks are visible to this day, serving as grim reminders to all that chance upon them of the grief, the agony, and the humility that awaits an erring navigator.

As the reader will soon discover, only selected shipwreck sagas and sea monster tales have been included in this book. Due to lack of space, time, documented information, and the difficulty in obtaining illustrations, numerous accounts of coastal shipwrecks and sea monster sightings have been omitted. Also, it is important to note, the shipwreck listings begin in the area of Pescadero Point and work their way south, ending at Pfeiffer Point of the famed Big Sur coast. The reader should also be aware that the great majority of shipwreck listings are of vessels that exceed 100 tons. In excluding vessels of lesser tonnage, most fishing boats and pleasure craft were, out of necessity, omitted.

Regardless of the countless hours of research that went into this work and the amount of checking and rechecking that was done, slight variations may appear as additional information comes to light. Nevertheless, it is hoped that with the numerous never before published photographs and the colorful accounts of central California's shipwrecks and sea monsters, this book will give each and every reader many hours of pleasure and will help to make them more aware of the remarkable history surrounding California's central coast.

ACKNOWLEDGEMENTS

I t would be difficult to list all the people who have helped to make this book become a reality. However, it would be extremely unjust if a limited few of these individuals were not singled out for a special word of praise and a hearty thank you.

On top of the list, and perhaps without whose help "Shipwrecks and Sea Monsters of California's Central Coast" would not have been completed, is A. E. M. "Max" Plapp. Much of the information contained in this book, and many of the pictures found on these pages, are from the Plapp collection. Always ready with an answer and eager to help in whatever way possible, the author is deeply indebted to this Pacific Grove gentleman who loves the sea and all that it represents.

A second name that deserves special mention is that of Matilda Dring of the San Francisco Maritime Museum. It was through Mrs. Dring's interest and effort that valuable information was obtained. Also, without her help this book would not boast nearly the number of illustrations that it does.

Other names, such as Admiral Earl Stone of Monterey's Allen Knight Maritime Museum, Rita Bottoms and Carol Champion of the Special Collections section of the University of California at Santa Cruz, Ruth Fisher of the Monterey County Library in Salinas, Charles Prentiss of the Santa Cruz City Museum, Ernest Hunter of the California State Department of Parks and Recreation, and Jessie Sandholdt of Monterey, have all played an important part in helping to make this book become a reality.

Add to this list the names of many of Monterey's veteran fishermen, numerous old-timers from up and down the central coast, and countless dedicated research librarians throughout the state, and one can begin to appreciate the vast number of people who were consulted in the preparation of this work. If it were not for the help received and the hundreds of aged newspapers, as well as the variety of publications that were made available to the author, many of the stories, and much of the detailed information contained on these pages, would not have been included in the finished work.

Finally, the author wishes to acknowledge the help and patience of his wife, Debbie, and his son, Erick, who helped in so many ways to bring "Shipwrecks and Sea Monsters of California's Central Coast" to completion.

SHIPWRECKS OF CALIFORNIA'S CENTRAL COAST

THIS MAP IS NOT MEANT TO SERVE AS
A SHIPWRECK GUIDE, AS THE LOCATIONS
SHOWN ARE ONLY APPROXIMATE.

Pescadero Point
1

2 3
Pigeon Point 4 5
7 6
Franklin Point 8
Point Ano Nuevo 9

Santa Cruz
10 11 14
12 13
Point Santa Cruz

Watsonville

15
Elkhorn Slough
16
17 Moss Landing
MONTEREY BAY 18

Salinas River

Point Pinos 19
23 22 20
24 21
Point Joe 25
26
27
Cypress Point 28 29
30
Point Lobos 31

Yankee Point

32
Ventura Rocks
Point Sur
34 33
35
36 37
Cooper Point 38
41 39 40
Pfeiffer Point

9

COVER ILLUSTRATION

The above scene shows the bow of the 2,477-ton lumber schooner HOWARD OLSON minutes before her death plunge off the Big Sur coast. She was the victim of a ramming by the 10,000-ton freighter MARINE LEOPARD, which resulted in the loss of the ship as well as the loss of four of her crew. A more complete account of the MARINE LEOPARD-HOWARD OLSON accident can be found on page 113. Additional pictures of this 1956 mishap are on pages 115-117.

The dramatic cover photograph was taken by Lee Blaisdell of Monterey, and has been reproduced through the courtesy of Monterey's Allen Knight Maritime Museum. Opened to the public in 1971, the museum has proved a popular attraction to both visitors and residents of the Monterey Peninsula. At present the museum is located in the heart of historic old Monterey (550 Calle Principal); however, future plans call for a more permanent location near Monterey's picturesque Fisherman's Wharf. Boasting countless maritime mementoes from ships that sailed the seven seas (plus numerous relics from ships that have been wrecked along California's central coast), the museum also lists among its outstanding displays the beautiful (and original) Fresenel Lenses of the Big Sur coast's Point Sur light station. Additional items of interest contained in the museum include a complete marine-oriented library, several elaborate and painstakingly-constructed models, and a picture collection that numbers in the thousands. Sponsored and supported by the Monterey History and Art Association, the museum is free to the public and is open every day except Monday.

SHIPWRECKS

TAMIAHUA

As mentioned in the introduction, the small community of Pescadero (located slightly inland from the coast) and the Pescadero shoreline mark the northernmost points discussed in "Shipwrecks and Sea Monsters of California's Central Coast." Located slightly north of historic Pigeon Point, the Pescadero shoreline and Pescadero Reef have, over the years, been the sites of several shipwrecks and coastal strandings.

Perhaps the most discussed, and certainly one of the largest vessels to have become stranded upon the Pescadero shore, was the Richfield Oil tanker TAMIAHUA.

Outbound from San Francisco and heading toward southern California, the TAMIAHUA groped her way through the night as a dense blanket of fog limited visibility to practically zero. Suddenly, and almost without warning, the 11,170-ton tanker struck Pescadero Reef and ground to a shuddering stop upon the sandy shore.

The date of the mishap was November 6, 1930, and despite the efforts of the tugs SEA ROVER, SEA RANGER and PEACOCK, as well as the assistance of the Coast Guard cutters CAHOKIA and SHAWNEE, the TAMIAHUA remained a captive of the Pescadero sand until the morning of November 25th. On that date, with the much needed assistance of an exceptionally high tide, the TAMIAHUA was pulled from the shore. Finally free of the captive sand, the TAMIAHUA was towed by the tug PEACOCK to the Moore Shipbuilding Company of San Francisco for repairs to her hull.

COLUMBIA

The July 14, 1896 wreck of the steamer COLUMBIA, approximately eight miles south of the Pescadero shoreline (listed in many sources as "off" Pigeon Point), is said to have had a profound effect on the tiny nearby community of Pescadero.

The COLUMBIA, of the Pacific Mail Steamship Company, was a

familiar sight to residents up and down the Pacific Coast as her regular run took her between San Francisco and the country of Panama. Built in 1892, she was still a relatively young vessel when she met her end on the fog-shrouded rocks of the California coast. Said to be on the verge of breaking the speed record for a run up the coast, the captain of the COLUMBIA reportedly chose to "defy" the ever present covering of summer fog, and instead of inching his way up the fog blanketed coast, he elected to trust his good judgment and make a run for the Golden Gate.

Of course there are two sides to almost every tale, and the CO-LUMBIA's captain told a different story. According to aged newspaper accounts, the captain "mistook" the mournful cry of the Pigeon Point foghorn for the sound of a passing ship, and, upon turning toward it (why he turned toward the sound of a passing ship has often been questioned), he drove his ship "almost into the lighthouse."

Whatever the reason, or perhaps the combination of the two, the 3,616-ton Panamanian steamer wound up on the rocks near treacherous Pigeon Point. Fortunately no lives were lost in the wreck, but the ship, as well as the cargo (which contained a large quantity of white lead paint) became a total loss. . . , at least to the owners of the Pacific Mail Steamship Company! Further accounts report a sudden transformation in the appearance of the nearby village of Pescadero, as, perhaps by coincidence, a goodly number of the buildings in this quaint California community soon "blossomed forth" in a summery coating of white paint!

CARRIER PIGEON

The historic distinction of being the first vessel to miss the Golden Gate and, instead, to meet her end on the rugged California coast, is bestowed upon the clipper ship CARRIER PIGEON. As was the case with so many ships that followed her lead and suffered similar fates upon the rocks, the CARRIER PIGEON was the victim of a dense California fog.

On her maiden voyage, the CARRIER PIGEON was 129 days out of Boston when she struck the rocks off what was then referred to as "Punta de la Ballena" (Whale Point) or "Cabo de Fortunas" (Cape of Adventure). Sources to this day disagree as to what month the fabled ship met her end (with the majority stating it was May), but all agree that the year was 1853. Sources are also a bit sketchy as to her exact tonnage (most accounts list her as having been in the 1,000 to 1,500-ton category), and are rather vague as to the number of lives that were lost in the long ago mishap (some accounts state numerous lives were lost, but the majority of reports indicate all hands reached shore safely).

Listed as having met her end a few miles north of Point Ano Nuevo, the ill-fated CARRIER PIGEON is described as having "come to rest amidship on a ledge of rocks which have broken the ship's back." Further reports state, "If Captain (Azariah) Doane had not had un-founded fears of salvage claims and had accepted the offered aid of the steamer ACTIVE, he might have saved the new ship and its cargo."

As it turned out, the ship (along with her beautifully carved figurehead of a pigeon) became a total loss, and, to make matters worse, additional accounts state the rescue ship SEA BIRD, which came to her aid from San Francisco, was also wrecked upon the shore of what soon became known as Pigeon Point. While not blessed with a long and colorful life upon the waterways of the world, nevertheless, the stately clipper ship CARRIER PIGEON has the distinction of lending her name to a portion of California's rugged coast, and, because of her wreck (as well as additional shipwrecks that were to follow), a lighthouse was erected upon the promontory that bears her name.

COYA

*A*dditional shipwrecks of note that have taken place in the vicin-ity of Pigeon Point include the British bark COYA which was wrecked off the fabled point in 1866. Out of Sydney, Australia, and bound for San Francisco, the COYA was also a victim of California's coastal fog.

Not having been able to plot their location for two days because of the dense fog, the survivors of the COYA disaster told of running by "dead reckoning" and thinking they were still a good distance from shore. Suddenly, in the early hours of the night, breakers were spotted, and before the ship could be turned away the COYA struck a reef and rolled over in relatively deep water. Heavily loaded with a cargo of coal, as well as a limited number of passengers, the COYA soon slipped under the sea. . . , carrying 27 of the 30 people aboard with her! The only survivors of this 1866 nightmare were two men and a boy who managed to reach the safety of shore and make their way to a nearby ranch.

The Richfield Oil Company tanker TAMIAHUA was a captive of the Pescadero sand for nineteen days after she ran aground in the fog on November 6, 1930. Refloated on November 25th, the TAMIAHUA was towed to San Francisco for repairs. Credit — Plapp Collection.

The Pennsylvania built COLUMBIA, owned by the Pacific Mail Steamship Company, was a victim of coastal fog and went aground near Pigeon Point on July 14, 1896. Fortunately no lives were lost in the mishap, but the trim four year old Panamanian steamer became a total loss. Credit — Alexander Moore photo — courtesy of the San Mateo County Historical Association and the San Francisco Maritime Museum.

After colliding with the Standard Oil Company tanker S.C.T. DODD in the shipping lanes off Pigeon Point, the veteran coastal liner SAN JUAN sank to the bottom of the Pacific. With 87 people losing their lives in this August 29, 1929 accident, the sinking of the 2,076-ton, 47-year old vessel ranks high on the list of California's most tragic maritime disasters. Credit — San Francisco Maritime Museum.

A waiting ambulance meets the S.C.T. DODD as she brings SAN JUAN survivors to San Francisco. Credit — San Francisco Maritime Museum.

The POINT ARENA, owned by the Beadle Steamship Company of San Francisco, went on the rocks at Pigeon Point on August 9, 1913, and became a total loss. The 223-ton lumber schooner is shown during happier days somewhere off the northern California coast. Credit – San Francisco Maritime Museum.

hellespont

The next Pigeon Point disaster to claim both a ship as well as a portion of her crew, took place a mere two years after the 1866 tragedy of the COYA.

The name of the vessel was the HELLESPONT, and the circumstances surrounding her wreck are remarkably similar to the circumstances surrounding the wreck of the COYA. Not only did she become a total loss and lose part of her crew, but the HELLESPONT is also said to have been of British registry, outbound from Australia, and carrying a cargo of coal when she hit the rocks of dreaded Pigeon Point.

The date of the disaster was November 19, 1868, and seven (some sources say eleven) members of the eighteen-man crew lost their lives to the angry sea. As the story goes, one member of the crew, "more dead than alive," crawled up a bluff and after much groping in the darkness, he stumbled upon a trail leading to a nearby Portuguese whaling village.

Bruised and bleeding, as well as having lost his clothes in his battle with the sea, the half-dead sailor managed to reach the village as a glint of dawn broke over the eastern hills. As he crept toward the entryway of the nearest cottage, a half-awake whaler met him at the door. Convinced he was looking into the face of a ghost, the terrified whaler turned and ran into the cottage, screaming as he went! Seeing a chance for help, and far too cold to speak, the half-dead mariner staggered after the frightened whaler. In his haste to flee the ghostly creature at his front door, the screaming whaler stumbled and fell headlong upon the cottage floor. Following his horrified host into the darkened room, the shipwrecked sailor stumbled upon the outstretched body of the stunned whaler and fell on top of him. Thinking his end had surely come, the terror-stricken whaler continued to scream and flail his arms about as the dead weight of the sailor pinned him down.

Hearing the commotion from the cottage, fellow whalers from throughout the village jumped from their beds and ran to the aid of their stricken comrade. Charging into the darkened cottage, the half-dressed whalers stumbled over the prostrate bodies upon the floor. . . , adding to the confusion and to the terror of the original whaler!

Finally, after cooler heads prevailed, and after the "rescuers" unwrapped themselves from the shipwrecked mariner, the half-dead sailor was sufficiently revived to tell his tale. In turn, when the unsuspecting whalers heard of the tragedy, they gathered their gear and headed for the beach, hoping to be of help to any remaining survivors

Finding bodies tossed to and fro and parts of the wrecked ship scattered up and down the shore, the whalers cared for the wounded and, with the aid of a telegraph station on the point (primarily used for communication with the Merchants' Exchange in San Francisco), they spread the word of the shipwreck up and down the coast.

SAN JUAN

While not a casualty of Pigeon Point, but taking place in the vicinity of her rocky promontory, the tragic story of the wreck of the SAN JUAN is a must for any book describing shipwrecks of the Pacific Coast. Being one of California's most discussed maritime disasters, the nightmare of the SAN JUAN took place in the shipping lanes off Pigeon Point on August 29, 1929.

Sailing under the banner of the Los Angeles-San Francisco Navigation Company, the veteran liner was on a routine coastal run when a blanket of fog dropped its familiar lid over the central California coast. With the combination of darkness and fog making navigation extremely hazardous, all ships in the area proceeded with extreme caution. Suddenly the eerie sound of an approaching ship's whistle was heard by those on the bridge of the SAN JUAN. As normal precautions were taken aboard the two oncoming vessels, the whistle signals were somehow misunderstood - - - resulting in a sickening crash and a death-dealing blow to the SAN JUAN! Nearly cutting the aged liner in half, the bow of the Standard Oil Company tanker S.C.T. DODD, is described as having inflicted a gash in the SAN JUAN's side large enough to drive a train through!

Suffering major damage to his own ship, the captain of the DODD reversed engines and slowly backed away from the stricken liner. As the DODD cleared the SAN JUAN, and water rushed in to fill the void, the severely damaged liner and her shaken passengers had but five minutes in which to "live." Unfortunately the great majority of the voyagers aboard the SAN JUAN were asleep in their bunks at the time of the collision. As the water rushed in and filled the bowels of the ship, these unfortunate souls were trapped in their quarters, not having a chance of escape.

Those who did manage to reach the deck had no time to lower

lifeboats or search out lifejackets as the crippled liner prepared for her death plunge. Braving the cold inky black of the Pacific, panicked passengers and dumbfounded crew members flung themselves into the fog-shrouded water, frantically grasping for anything that would keep them afloat.

As the SAN JUAN slipped beneath the Pacific, the crippled DODD stood by to pick up survivors. In addition to the DODD, the steamer MUNAMI, which had been in the vicinity at the time of the collision, picked up a distress signal and hurried to the scene of the accident. After searching the area through the long night and well into the next day, the final tally of survivors totaled a meager 42 (31 aboard the DODD and 11 aboard the MUNAMI). This final tally left 87 people unaccounted for! Eighty-seven lost souls. . . , the majority of whom were entombed in the broken hull of the SAN JUAN as she sank to the bottom of the sea!

Perhaps at this point a final note should be added to this tragic tale, as according to a noted authority on lost Pacific treasures, the hull of the 283-foot SAN JUAN lies at a depth of twelve fathoms (72 feet), and contains approximately $200,000 in unclaimed treasure (mostly of the gold and silver variety)! With this in mind, perhaps instead of death, destruction, and despair, the tale of the SAN JUAN may hold the key to "instant wealth" for some future treasure seeker. But, regardless of treasure, or any other colorful anecdote that is told of the sinking of the SAN JUAN, nothing can detract from the morbid fact that the loss of this coastal liner has gone down in history as one of California's worst maritime disasters.

POINT ARENA

M any of the vessels that met their end on or in the vicinity of Pigeon Point, were not of the headline making variety. While the wrecks were just as real and the loss of life was just as tragic, nevertheless, the wrecks of the small coastal freighters and the picturesque lumber schooners did not gain the public's attention as did the mishaps involving larger vessels.

The wreck of the POINT ARENA is a prime example. Although there was no loss of life, and the story of the wreck and the plight of the people aboard may not have been as dramatic as the events surrounding the collision of the SAN JUAN, nevertheless, vessels of the POINT

ARENA variety – often referred to as the work-horses of the Pacific Coast – are certainly worthy of mention.

Although information regarding the cause of her wreck is sketchy, we do know the POINT ARENA was a steam schooner of 223 tons; she was built in San Francisco; she served in the coastal lumber trade for many years as well as spending considerable time (during the 1890's) plying the waters between Vancouver Island (Canada) and the mainland; and, finally, she met her end on Pigeon Point on August 9, 1913.

SIR JOHN FRANKLIN

A pproximately halfway between Pigeon Point and Point Ano Nuevo lies Franklin Point, a second promontory that gained its name from a ship that died upon its rocks. The sleek nine-year veteran of ocean runs that "christened" it with this name was the American-built SIR JOHN FRANKLIN. Described as a medium clipper ship (boasting more sail than the usual merchantman of her day), the 999-ton FRANKLIN was outbound from Baltimore and heading toward the Golden Gate when fog and heavy seas combined to seal her doom.

Before reaching the California coast, aged records tell of the FRANKLIN calling at the Atlantic port of Rio de Janeiro. At this South American port she discharged a portion of her cargo, and took on added freight, before continuing her voyage. Berthed in this famed Brazilian harbor at the time of the FRANKLIN's visit was the ship CHARLES L. PENNEL, which had been condemned as unseaworthy by port authorities. With the PENNEL also loaded with a cargo bound for far-off San Francisco, Captain John Dupeaux of the FRANKLIN and a business representative of the PENNEL's owners worked out an agreement enabling the FRANKLIN to take a portion of the PENNEL's cargo to the Golden Gate.

So. . . , with a full cargo, containing such things as dry goods, lumber, pianos, and 300 barrels of "spirits," the SIR JOHN FRANKLIN rounded South America and fought its way up the Pacific Coast – only to be cast upon the rocks of a then unnamed point.

According to survivors of this 1865 tragedy, the FRANKLIN had been "lost" in a dense fog and had been fighting a heavy sea for 24 hours before the mishap occurred. Even though it was next to impossible to accurately judge their exact position, Captain Dupeaux was of the opinion they were "far out to sea" when breakers were suddenly spotted crashing upon the nearby shore. Every effort was made to gain open water, but three times in succession the pounding waves caught the ship and threw her on the rocks. The third time she was cast upon the rocks the FRANKLIN parted amidship and her cargo, as well as her dazed crew, were spilled into the water.

Captain Dupeaux and twelve of his men lost their lives on that fateful January day, leaving only three of the crew to cheat the angry sea and live to tell the story of the last voyage of the SIR JOHN FRANKLIN.

It is of interest to note that San Francisco owners of the 300 barrels of "spirits" sent a small army of law officers to visit residents of the Franklin Point area, hoping against hope to retrieve at least a portion of their lost cargo. But. . . , perhaps as would be expected. . . , not one of the "Franklinites" questioned could shed any light on the mysterious disappearance of the 300 barrels of booze!

J.W. SEAVER

Punta de Ano Nuevo boasts a recorded history dating back to 1603. On January 3rd of that long-ago year the famed Basque navigator, Sebastian Viscaino, christened it Point of the New Year in honor of its being the first promontory he spotted that year. Today, more than three and a half centuries later, Point Ano Nuevo boasts an interesting history of coastal shipwrecks.

Perhaps of most interest to Pacific shipwreck enthusiasts is the relatively new story of a very old wreck. Taking place on April 10, 1887, and being little more than a legend to the people of the Point Ano Nuevo area, the actual account of the wreck of the J. W. SEAVER was not brought to light until 1965. The man responsible for this fascinating tale is Henry Bradley, of Coastways Ranch in southern San Mateo County. While strolling a storm-wracked Ano Nuevo beach one day in 1964, Bradley found a large iron ring of "nautical nature" that turned out to be the key that unlocked an aged Pacific Coast mystery.

Curious as to what kind of maritime memento he had found, and vaguely remembering rambling tales of a ship called the J. W. SEAVER that wrecked on an Ano Nuevo shore, Bradley took his find to the San

Francisco Maritime Museum to see if, by chance, it could have been from that long-ago wreck. Having little trouble discovering his relic was a "bowsprit band," used by ships of the J. W. SEAVER type, Bradley and the museum staff had considerably more trouble in attempting to discover what had become of the J. W. SEAVER. In checking through what is considered to be the most complete shipwreck file on the Pacific Coast, the closest any of the staff could come to pinpointing the end of the J. W. SEAVER, was the fact that the vessel had mysteriously dropped from the ships' registry after 1887!

With that as a starter, Bradley returned to his Ano Nuevo home and, when time permitted, he made annual pilgrimages to Santa Cruz where he pored through aged copies of the Daily Surf. Finally, in an issue dated April 12, 1887, Bradley found an account of the shipwreck of the J. W. SEAVER – complete with a narrative from the lost ship's captain!

With this 1965 find, the 78-year old mystery of the disappearance of the J. W. SEAVER was solved, and, perhaps of even more importance, with the account of the J. W. SEAVER's wreck upon the shore of Point Ano Nuevo, the history of shipwrecks along the central California coast becomes one step closer to being complete.

According to the 1887 account, the J. W. SEAVER was a bark and had been built in Chelsea, Massachusetts, about 1860. Before coming to the Pacific Coast, she had spent many years in the West Indies trade. At the time of her wreck her cargo consisted of approximately 10 tons of salt and 60 tons of hay.

The narrative of Captain Robert Robertson is of interest as it describes the plight of the J. W. SEAVER as it died upon the shore:

"When we were off Ano Nuevo Island the lee side of the deck was under water and I saw that we could not keep afloat long, so hoping to save life and property, I stood in for the beach. We struck at 9 a.m., a strong wind was blowing and a heavy surf was rolling in, breaking over the ship fore and aft. We attempted to launch the boat, but it was immediately smashed to atoms. Nothing more could be done and I told the men that we must watch our chance and get ashore as we could on pieces of the vessel.

"Immediately after we struck she commenced to go to pieces, and every breaker took away some of the cargo and parts of the vessel, and soon the water in shore was a mass of floating wreckage."

What Captain Robertson's report failed to mention, was that a rescue party of spirited citizens tied ropes around their waists and risked their lives in valiant attempts to help crew members of the J. W. SEAVER fight their way through the mountainous breakers. Five of the crew reaped the benefits of the "local heroics," but a sad five they were as three of their shipmates lost their lives to the angry sea.

As to what became of the iron memento that once graced the bow of the J. W. SEAVER, it, along with the account of the 1887 shipwreck, was presented to the San Francisco Maritime Museum. Thanks to the persistence and dedication of Henry Bradley, shipwreck enthusiasts up and down the coast can now fill in the void after the name J. W. SEAVER.

CRESCENT CITY

Slightly south of Point Ano Nuevo is the northern entrance to Monterey Bay. Included in the history of this world-renowned bay is a list of shipwrecks dating back to the early 1830's.

In describing a selected number of these mishaps, it will become evident to the reader that vessels of all shapes and sizes have met their ends upon the shores of this rounded bay. Heading the list of shipwrecks that have taken place near the north coast community of Santa Cruz is the steam schooner CRESCENT CITY. A victim of heavy fog, the CRESCENT CITY came to grief approximately four miles north of the Santa Cruz lighthouse on July 7, 1927. Enroute to Monterey at the time of the mishap, the 642-ton vessel was scheduled to pick up a load of Monterey's famed sardines.

Built in 1906 at Aberdeen, Washington, the CRESCENT CITY served for many years under the name JIM BUTLER. Under this name she was used extensively as a lumber freighter and made many voyages up and down the coast. At the time of her loss she was described as a coastal freighter with her main run being between Monterey and San Francisco.

The stranded 642-ton coastal lumber schooner CRESCENT CITY. On her way to Monterey the vessel became lost in a dense fog and went aground approximately four miles north of Lighthouse Point near Santa Cruz. The accident occured on July 7, 1927, and the twenty-one year old vessel became a total loss.

Credit — Allen Knight Maritime Museum.

Credit — Plapp Collection.

The three photographs on these pages graphically illustrate the wreck of the small coastal freighter LA FELIZ. She came to grief approximately two miles north of the Santa Cruz light station, and was soon a total loss. Heavy seas were blamed for the October 1, 1924 wreck, and her crew of thirteen was saved by heroic efforts of people on shore. Credit — Santa Cruz City Museum

Credit — Dorothy C. Miller

Credit — Dorothy C. Miller

27

Lighthouse Point, near Santa Cruz and along Monterey Bay's north shore, was the site of this October 26, 1876 stranding. High seas were blamed for the grounding, and the schooner ACTIVE became a total loss. Credit – Special Collections, University of California at Santa Cruz.

With the waves breaking around her, the beautiful SHAMROCK (officially known as the SHAMROCK VI) sits serenely in the surf on Santa Cruz beach. A victim of winds gusting up to 70 knots, the luxury yacht was blown ashore on October 7, 1972. Eventually refloated, after being battered by the sea for nearly a month, the elegant vessel finally gave in to the Pacific as she was being towed to a San Francisco Bay drydock. Credit – Jerry Draeger photo.

LA FELIZ

Among the coastal freighters that made frequent runs between San Francisco and the Bay of Monterey was the 102-ton vessel LA FELIZ. Unlike numerous other coastal freighters whose "bones" dot the shore near the southern extremities of Monterey Bay, the LA FELIZ, as did the CRESCENT CITY, met its fate on the north shore of the rounded bay.

Having left Monterey with a full load of canned sardines (3,100 cases) in the early evening of October 1, 1924, the captain of the 72-foot craft pointed the bow of his vessel toward her home port of San Francisco and dutifully headed for the Golden Gate. Heavy swells were running as the crew of the freighter fought their way across the bay and, as she neared the Santa Cruz coast, reports tell of her following a course too close to the rocky shore. Nearing Swanton Beach (also known as Moore's Beach – approximately one mile north of what is now known as the Natural Bridges State Park), the tiny freighter was caught in the heavy seas and unceremoniously dashed against an outcropping of rock.

With the site of the wreck directly below a jagged north coast cliff, and with the waves and heavy swells unmercifully pounding the ill-fated freighter, the rescue of the ship's crew proved extremely hazardous and not without its share of heroes.

When a line was finally secured to the stranded vessel, and when the crew of thirteen had safely made their way to shore, plans for salvage operations began to take shape.

As dawn broke and the seas subsided, groups of curious spectators began making their way to Swanton Beach to view the grounded freighter. With these early arrivals being rewarded with cans of sardines that had slipped through a gaping hole in the ship's hull, "local" interest in the wreck was heightened considerably. As the word "fish for the taking" spread throughout the north bay, a steady procession of visitors began arriving at the shipwreck site to claim their share of sardines.

As visitors continued to reap the harvest of "beached sardines," organized salvage operations went into high gear. Battling the breakers and the high seas, crew members of the LA FELIZ sought to recover machinery that was still serviceable, as well as the many cases of sardines that were still aboard the vessel.

In a matter of days all serviceable equipment had been removed from the ship, and the hold of the freighter had been emptied of its cargo. With the sardines gone, so disappeared the people — leaving the broken and beached LA FELIZ to die a lonely death among the combers of Monterey Bay's north shore.

ACTIVE

The year of the United States centennial celebration was also the year the schooner ACTIVE became stranded at Lighthouse Point, near Santa Cruz. The exact date of this century-old mishap was October 26, 1876.

Loaded with a cargo of 3,000 railroad ties (taken aboard at the old railroad wharf near Santa Cruz), the ACTIVE had no more than cleared port and made ready for a run to San Francisco when she became becalmed off Lighthouse Point. Upon dropping anchor to await a favorable breeze, the men of the ACTIVE found to their displeasure that instead of a breeze, the early morning hours brought storm-fed waves and a strong drift. At approximately 4:00 a.m., the anchor chains parted and the ACTIVE began drifting toward the shore, soon to become stranded upon Lighthouse Point beach.

Upon her grounding, the vessel remained upright, enabling her crew of seven to make a relatively easy escape. But, due to her heavy cargo, combined with the force in which she was thrown upon the sand, the vessel suffered extensive damage to her hull and was judged unsalvageable.

After members of the Adna Hecox family (lighthouse keepers from 1870 to 1919) assisted the crew up forty-foot cliffs and away from their beached vessel, owners of the ACTIVE were notified of her plight and plans to salvage her cargo were set in motion.

It was not long before the railroad ties were salvaged, but as an aged Santa Cruz newspaper reports, "the ACTIVE was active no more!"

SHAMROCK VI

Within the memory of most Monterey Bay area residents is the October 7, 1972, stranding of the luxury yacht SHAMROCK VI. Listed as a two-masted gaff-rigged schooner, the SHAMROCK was driven onto the Santa Cruz beach by a sudden squall that registered winds gusting up to 70 knots!

Fronting the boardwalk and within a "stone's throw" of the Municipal Wharf, the 2:30 p.m. grounding of the SHAMROCK was witnessed by hundreds of Saturday afternoon sight-seers. Remaining upright, the mahogany paneled and teakwood decked yacht was described as being a "picture of elegance" even upon the sand. But, unbeknownst to the many spectators, the sudden squall that sent the ship ashore all but sealed the doom of the sixty-seven year old vessel. Owner, Dr. Jeremiah J. Wolohan of San Francisco, reported that the SHAMROCK was moored in the Santa Cruz harbor because of engine trouble and that he and a mechanic had been working on the engine only a few minutes before the squall hit. Leaving the mechanic and his wife and two small children aboard the vessel, Wolohan made a quick trip to the Santa Cruz yacht harbor to pick up some parts for the engine.

Upon his return, approximately fifteen minutes later, Wolohan was shocked to find his ship on the beach! Lacking power to reach the safety of deep water, the gale force winds had driven the picturesque yacht toward the shore — anchor and all! Nearing the beach, the wind spun the SHAMROCK around as if she were a toy and drove her high onto the sand. Fortunately no one was injured as the vessel struck the Santa Cruz shore, and the four people aboard the stricken craft made an orderly exit once the boat came to rest.

Although besieged with calls, as the sudden squall had played havoc with many boats around the bay, the Coast Guard cutter POINT CHICO was soon upon the scene. Working for many hours, the dedicated crew of the POINT CHICO made several attempts to pull the SHAMROCK from the beach, but all attempts failed and the sleek yacht remained a captive of the Santa Cruz sand.

As Saturday turned to Sunday, and after several additional attempts by the Coast Guard, as well as by the tugboat LO-EV, failed to budge the SHAMROCK from her landlocked berth, the once bright future of the trim schooner began to look cloudy. By Monday, Dr. Wolohan, master of the yacht for 23 years, sensed the end of his proud vessel was near and made one last inspection tour of the stranded craft. Finding leaks throughout her sleek hull and water flooding her once elegant interior, Wolohan felt the SHAMROCK would sail no more and sadly sold the vessel to Rocco Cardinale (of nearby Salinas) for the sum of $5,000.

Cardinale, an electric motor repairman, had fallen in love with the grounded craft and was willing to gamble that she was not dead yet.

In hiring Moss Landing marine salvager Ben Hord, the drama of the SHAMROCK began to mount. Bringing his skill, his tractor, and a trained crew to the Santa Cruz beach, Ben Hord and his men began an all-out effort to save the beached vessel. Working day and night for nearly a month, these dedicated salvagers tried every effort imaginable in their attempts to free the stranded schooner. As their efforts continued to mount, and as the story of the SHAMROCK continued to make news, people from throughout central California ventured to the Santa Cruz waterfront to offer their advice or to just stand quietly and watch the salvagers as they went about their work.

Finally, at 8:25 on the morning of November 3rd, with the aid of a high tide, a bulldozer pushing from the shore, and a tugboat and a fishing boat pulling from the sea, the once captive SHAMROCK slid from the sand and bobbed in the water of Santa Cruz harbor! In the wild celebration that followed, people on shore cheered, car horns honked, and a bottle of champagne was poured over Ben Hord's head.

With pumps shooting water from her "innards," the once doomed schooner was a picture of loveliness to Rocco Cardinale and Ben Hord. Riding in the harbor until mid-afternoon, the SHAMROCK was inspected and judged capable of withstanding a trip to the Oakland estuary, where she had a much needed date with a drydock! Taken in tow by the San Francisco based tug LUCKY DAY II, the SHAMROCK began her last journey.

Making it to within a few miles of the Golden Gate, the ill-fated schooner, taking water and battered by heavy seas and high winds, could take no more and gave in to the unrelenting sea. In a final effort to save her, a Coast Guard cutter, a helicopter, and fixed winged aircraft were summoned to her aid, but because of high seas, only the helicopter could deliver a "life-saving" pump. Unfortunately one pump was not enough, and at 4:40 a.m., on November 4th, the SHAMROCK slipped from sight, bringing to a close the remarkable tale of a recent shipwreck and a gallant effort to help her live again.

PALO ALTO

O ver the years, perhaps the most talked about ship of the entire central California coast has been the broken and beached hulk of the once proud PALO ALTO.

Situated on Monterey Bay's north shore, the 435-foot hull of the PALO ALTO is, to this day, the main attraction of popular Seacliff State Beach. Towed to her Seacliff Beach mooring during the depression year of 1930, the impressive vessel was little more than a decade old and soon became a sight-seeing must for the people of the Monterey Bay area.

Built of concrete, the PALO ALTO was designed as a tanker, and constructed by the United States government. The idea behind the building of cement ships was an attempt to ease the steel shortage at a time when the United States was in the midst of the First World War.

With the war over by the time the PALO ALTO was ready to test her sea legs, her May 29, 1919 launching did not create the fanfare a ship of her size would have ordinarily created. After sliding from her cradle at the Government Island Concrete Shipyard (between the San Francisco Bay communities of Oakland and Alameda), the 7,500-ton vessel became an immediate "white elephant" (perhaps "white whale" would be more appropriate), and was destined to spend the next ten years along the Oakland waterfront.

Eventually purchased by the Cal-Nevada Company (composed primarily of Nevada businessmen) for a fraction of her original $1,500, 000 cost, the PALO ALTO was stripped of her machinery and towed to her permanent home along Monterey Bay's north shore.

Having purchased 500 feet of beach frontage along the Seacliff waterfront, the Cal-Nevada Company had the PALO ALTO's lengthy hull moored a short distance from shore, with her bow pointing toward the distant Monterey Peninsula. A 600-foot pier was soon constructed and a $500,000, six-month job of remodeling and refitting the vessel was begun. Included in the half-million dollar project was the filling of six of the ship's storage tanks with sand. Serving as ballast, the sand "insured" the vessel would remain a permanent fixture.

Upon completion of the remodeling job, the once-forgotten and oft-neglected tanker began life anew as an amusement center. Containing approximately 68,000 feet of deck space, the "new" PALO ALTO boasted such things as a heated swimming pool, an immense ballroom, an elaborate cafe, a dining saloon (mounted in the ship's superstructure), carnival concessions, and an abundance of deck space for the fishing enthusiast.

With over 3,000 people attending its opening ceremonies, which included a grand ball, the PALO ALTO's new lease on life looked as though it would be a long and profitable one. Unfortunately, after only two seasons — amid rumors of bootlegging (as Prohibition was still in effect) and gambling — the owners of the PALO ALTO declared bankruptcy, leaving the twice-forsaken cement ship to the elements and the fishermen.

Withering in the agony of her misfortunes, and being severely battered by the winds and waves of Monterey Bay, the PALO ALTO did not last through the following winter as a severe crack was discovered in her hull. What was still salvageable aboard the forsaken vessel was soon removed and sold, an example being a portion of the wooden superstructure which found its way to nearby Santa Cruz, where it served as a tire warehouse until the mid 1960's.

As the winter storms came and went the gallant vessel was the target of storm-fed winds and angry waves. Eventually breaking amidship, the bow section of the vessel settled forward on the uneven floor of Monterey Bay, forcing a catwalk to be built to connect the two sections. Continuing to serve in this manner as a haven for fishermen and for those interested in nautical oddities, the broken-hulled PALO ALTO remained a must for visitors to Monterey Bay's north shore.

In 1936 the State purchased the vessel and "all thereon" for the sum of one dollar. In 1958 the bow section of the vessel was declared unsafe and a fence was built where the catwalk once stood. In 1963 a fierce Pacific storm nearly severed the bow, causing considerable concern as to the fate of both the bow and stern sections of the ship.

But . . . , as storms continue to come and go, and nearly half a century since the PALO ALTO opened its doors and welcomed 3,000 visitors to its gala "welcome aboard" party, the broken and beached tanker continues to greet thousands of annual visitors. Not as elegant as she once was, and certainly not serving the purpose she was created for, nevertheless, the PALO ALTO remains the star attraction of California's state-owned Seacliff Beach.

Labeled as a general progress view, the PALO ALTO begins to take shape at the Government Concrete Shipyard in Oakland, California. Credit — San Francisco Maritime Museum.

The cement ship PALO ALTO as she appeared on the day of her launching, May 29, 1919. Credit — San Francisco Maritime Museum.

Boasting the title of the world's largest concrete tanker, the imposing PALO ALTO goes to drydock for cleaning, painting and minor repairs to her hull. This photograph was taken at the Moore Shipbuilding Company in Oakland, California, June 18, 1920. Credit — San Francisco Maritime Museum.

After being purchased by the Cal-Nevada Company the 7,500-ton vessel was towed to Seacliff Beach where she was moored near the shore. Taken in 1930, this photograph shows the PALO ALTO before the 600-foot pier was constructed. Credit — California State Department of Parks and Recreation.

With the completion of the PALO ALTO's six-month remodeling job, the trim lines of a tanker were all but lost as the cement ship was transformed into an amusement center. Credit — California State Department of Parks and Recreation.

The cliffs of Seacliff Beach, or Sea Cliff Park, as the area was then known, afforded visitors a bird's eye view of the PALO ALTO and the 600-foot pier that led to her. Credit — California State Department of Parks and Recreation.

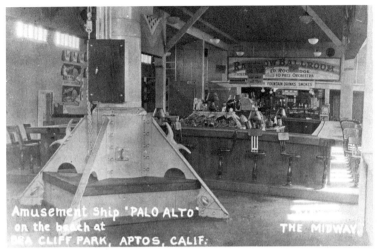

In this view of the "midway" aboard the amusement ship PALO ALTO, one can see a sign advertising the Rainbow Ballroom, where long-ago residents of Monterey Bay's north shore danced to the ten-piece orchestra of Ed Rookledge. Credit — California State Department of Parks and Recreation.

A pause in the music affords the photographer a chance to "capture the couples" as they await conductor Ed Rookledge to once again strike up the band. The Rainbow Ballroom measured 156 feet in length and 54 feet in width, and was a popular gathering place during the PALO ALTO's short two-year tenure as an amusement ship. Credit — California State Department of Parks and Recreation.

F-1

As previously mentioned, the historic bay of Monterey boasts a considerable collection of shipwrecks and strandings. In researching into the numerous mishaps of this central California bay, many interesting incidents and colorful dramas have come to light. However, the accounts of many of the aged incidents are somewhat sketchy and therefore the events leading up to the mishaps, as well as the details of the mishaps themselves, may never be fully known.

Fortunately for history buffs with an eye toward the unusual, the story of an odd and somewhat tragic shipwreck in a Monterey Bay port — that is no more — was accurately reported and duly recorded in the year of 1912.

The ship involved in this long-ago mishap makes the story of even more interest as it was none other than a rare (in 1912) United States submarine, the very same submarine that held the world's depth record of 280 feet, which it had only recently set in the confines of San Francisco Bay.

The harbor involved in this rather strange maritime drama makes the story even more unique, as the events took place at the now defunct port of Watsonville (an inland Monterey Bay community). In checking into the details of this early 1900 shipwreck, one finds that near the turn of the century the apple growing community of Watsonville was in the habit of staging an annual "Apple Festival." The idea behind this Pajaro Valley extravaganza was to focus attention on the apple industry of southern Santa Cruz County.

Festivities enjoyed by the hundreds of people who thronged to the "Annuals" took place at the bustling valley community as well as at her somewhat distant harbor. Among the port activities of the 1912 event was the advertised inauguration of a new steamer service from San Francisco to Watsonville. This, accompanied by daily baseball games on the beach, fishing, dancing, numerous concessions, and the thrill of riding an electric car line from the town to the shore, all combined to create quite a hubbub of activity in the community as well as at her distant beach. As if these events were not enough, the U.S. cruiser ALERT and the submarines F-1 and F-2 were scheduled to visit Port Watsonville during the festival.

As the days ticked by, the "Apple Annual" boasted large crowds as people from all corners of the state visited California's "Apple City" to view the colorful displays and take part in the many activities. As the record crowds enjoyed the numerous events and thrilled to the sight of the proud warships, the day of departure for Uncle Sam's mini-fleet rapidly drew near. However, much to the dismay of Watsonville's shocked citizenry, fate had other plans in store for the Navy's record-setting submarine.

In the pre-dawn hours of October eleventh (one day before the vessels were due to depart), the tragedy of the F–1 began to unfold. As the submarines lay at anchor near the Port Watsonville pier, the early morning hours brought heavy swells and high rolling breakers to the curving shoreline of Monterey Bay. With the seas continuing to rise, the submarines strained at their anchor cables as they pitched and rolled in the heavy seas. At approximately 4:00 a.m., the anchor cable of the F–1 (which was attached to a harbor buoy) could stand the strain no longer! Giving in to a mighty wave, the cable suddenly snapped, leaving the F–1 at the mercy of the heavy swells and pounding breakers.

With her anchor cable gone, the helpless submarine is reported to have been "swept ashore with incredible speed!" Grounding on the beach near the Port Watsonville pier, the shuddering jar of her sudden stop shook the sleeping members of the F–1's crew from their bunks. Chief Electrician W. M. Young raced to the switchboard in a frantic effort to start the engines and free the ship from the captive sands. But, even as the engines caught, it was obvious to all aboard that the F–1 would need assistance if she were to be freed from the vise-like grip of the Watsonville sand.

Climbing the ladder inside the sub's conning tower, Seamen James Turbett and Gustave Schroeder were the first to reach the bridge of the disabled ship (located approximately four feet above the tapered deck). A quote from the Watsonville Evening Pajaronian (October 11, 1912) graphically records the tragic results of Turbett and Schroeder's climb up the conning tower ladder; "As the two men reached the bridge, the breakers which were sweeping one after the other over the decks and top of the boat, seized the two men and carried them out into the water. Those on board that rushed to the rescue saw Turbett attempt to gain the boat again only to be swept away. The condition of his body when found indicates that he was struck by an object, probably the buoy, and killed by the blow. His body was washed upon the sands. Schroeder was swept out upon the seas and probably drowned."

As tragic as these two deaths were, it is fortunate that there were only two seamen who lost their lives. With the waves continuing to batter the helpless submarine and embed it ever deeper into the sand, the fate of the remaining fourteen men aboard the vessel was constantly in doubt.

The first person on shore to realize something was amiss was the night watchman for the Watsonville Railway and Navigation Company. Peering through the darkness of a thick Monterey Bay fog, he spotted the stranded submarine and hastily notified port authorities. In the meantime the siren of the F–1 had been activated and screamed a signal of distress – arousing crew members aboard the F–2 and the ALERT (including Lieutenant J. B. Howell, the captain of the F–1, who had been quartered for the night aboard the cruiser).

The large whaleboat of the ALERT was immediately lowered and soon was heading toward the stranded submarine. Realizing the danger they too were in, the men of the F–2 fired up their engines and pointed the bow of their vessel toward the deep water, eventually being secured near their convoy leader, the cruiser ALERT. (One unconfirmed 1912 account tells of the F–2 being battered against the Port Watsonville pier by the heavy swells and crashing waves before she was finally able to gain the open sea.)

As the crew of the whaleboat battled the waves in an effort to reach the hapless submarine, the fourteen remaining members of the F–1's crew did all that was humanly possible to free their vessel from the sand. Finally, all hope was exhausted and there was little left for the men to do but hope and pray that they would be rescued. As the men aboard the whaleboat braved the angry waters of Monterey Bay, the crew of the F–1 counted the minutes as the pounding breakers continued to buffet the sub and roll it from side to side as if it were a toy.

All too soon it became obvious to the men of the F–1 that it would be suicide to stay below decks any longer. Water was pouring in from the conning tower and escaping gas fumes were beginning to fill the inner compartments. With life preservers secured, one by one the men ventured up the conning tower ladder and onto the narrow deck. As the minutes continued to tick by and the heavy covering of fog cloaked the entire scene in inky black, the men were faced with a life and death decision. Some chose to risk their lives and attempted to swim to the Port Watsonville beach. Others chose to cling to the railing of the sub in hopes the whaleboat would soon appear and a rescue attempt could be made.

Those who chose to wait aboard the F–1 were soon rewarded, as within minutes the whaleboat appeared through the blanket of black and the heroic crew members of the rescue boat proceeded to pluck the men from the cold dark water. Those who attempted to reach the beach also succeeded in their efforts, but reports tell of them collapsing from exhaustion as they staggered from the angry sea. By 8:00 a.m., all but two of the fourteen crew members had been rescued. The two who were still unaccounted for had elected to stay aboard the submarine and could be seen bracing themselves against the conning tower as the waves crashed around them. Finally, at 10:30 a.m., they signalled to be taken ashore. Upon being rescued they were found to be in a state of shock as well as in serious physical condition (R. Ryan, one of the last two men to be rescued, is also reported to have been unconscious at the time of the rescue).

As the news of the tragedy of the F–1 spread to the communities surrounding Monterey Bay, officials of the "Apple Annual" hurriedly met and cancelled all events scheduled for Port Watsonville, including a smoker that had been scheduled for that evening, which was to have been in honor of the officers of Uncle Sam's mini-fleet.

With the F–1 continuing to be pounded by the breakers, spectators from near and far arrived at Port Watsonville to view the stranded vessel. As the multitude of spectators stared at the beach-bound ship, word circulated through the crowd that no attempt to free the sub would be made until a Navy tug arrived from the Mare Island Naval Shipyard (located near Vallejo, in San Francisco Bay).

With the Navy tug IROQUOIS due to arrive after dark, the first all-out effort to pull the F–1 from the sand was officially scheduled for the morning of October 12th. As the morning of the 12th dawned, the men of the IROQUOIS began the task of pulling the stranded submarine from the beach. But, as darkness came to Monterey Bay, the sub was still a captive of the Port Watsonville sand, although the crew of the IROQUOIS did manage to right the vessel and turn it half-way around, pointing the bow of the crippled ship toward the open sea.

When it became evident that additional help would be needed if the F–1 was to be freed, three additional tugs from Mare Island were summoned. It was not long before the IROQUOIS was joined by the tugs VIGILANTE, ACTIVE, and the UMATILLA. With October 13th and 14th coming and going, and with no noticeable movement of the stranded submarine to be observed, the might of the cruiser ALERT was added to the combined strength of the four Navy tugs. . . , only to be greeted with the same sad results!

The 15th of October brought word that the heavy cruiser MARYLAND had been intercepted as she steamed down the California coast and was scheduled to arrive in Monterey Bay on the 16th. When news reached the men of the F−1 that the MARYLAND (one of the Navy's largest cruisers) was coming to their aid, a feeling of optimism spread throughout the crew as they felt, with the might of the MARYLAND on their side, it wouldn't be long before the F−1 would again be seaborn.

It wasn't until around noon of the 16th that the MARYLAND steamed majestically into Monterey Bay. As midday came and went, and with the tide progressively dropping as each afternoon hour passed, concentrated efforts by the fleet of rescue ships were postponed until the following day. October 17th brought cheers and hope to the men of the F−1 as the cruiser MARYLAND, with the aid of the tug IROQUOIS, succeeded in pulling the submarine partially clear of the clinging sand.

Instead of cheers, the 18th of October only brought further frustration, as with the morning and evening high tides the tow lines to the stranded submarine proved unworthy of the task they had been chosen for. Breaking under the strain of the pull from the mighty MARYLAND, the F−1 was destined to remain a captive of the Watsonville sand for still another day.

The cheers that had been pent up by the weary crew of the F−1, as well as the hundreds of spectators who had maintained an eight-day vigil along the shores of Port Watsonville, finally burst forth at 7:20 on the morning of October 19, 1912. With heavier tow lines attached, combined with a morning high tide and a team effort by the men of the MARYLAND and the crews of the tugs VIGILANTE and IROQUOIS, the record-setting submarine was pulled from the sand and once again bobbed freely in the open sea!

Secured near her convoy escort, a thorough inspection of the F−1 was made. With all in agreement, and feeling the sub was capable of withstanding a trip to the Mare Island shipyard, the pride of the Pacific's submarine fleet departed the waters of Monterey Bay (under tow), one week and one day after she had become a prisoner of the Port Watsonville sand. Estimates at the time of her departure placed the cost of refitting the gallant F−1 in the $75,000 bracket − quite possibly the highest price ever paid for a goodwill visit to a port that is no more − to help celebrate an event that is no longer held!

The F — 1 as she appeared after her October 11, 1912 stranding. With the light of day, calm waters and a low tide, the record-setting submarine appears to be in relatively good condition as she rests high and dry upon the Port Watsonville sand. Credit — Pajaro Valley Historical Society.

Securing a line to the F — 1, crew members prepare to attempt to dislodge the 350-ton vessel. Credit — Pajaro Valley Historical Society.

With lines secured, and men from the F — 2 and the ALERT to help, a gallant attempt to dislodge the F — 1 is made. Note the elegant attire of many of the spectators as they mill about the beach and watch the straining seamen try to break the strangle-hold of the Port Watsonville sand. Credit — Pajaro Valley Historical Society.

A second view of the 1912 "tug-o-war." Unfortunately, the sands of Port Watsonville won this round as the might of the men could not match the suction-like pull of the sand. Note the horses on the beach, appearing to be quite interested in the proceedings, and perhaps wondering why they are not allowed to take part in the festivities. Also, shown in the background is the cruiser ALERT, the submarine F − 2, and three of the Mare Island tugboats. Credit − Pajaro Valley Historical Society.

With the "tug-o-war" over and the F − 1 still stuck, this 1912 photograph shows a handful of spectators, a portion of the Port Watsonville pier, as well as several vessels including the ALERT, the F − 2, and tugboats from Mare Island. Credit − Pajaro Valley Historical Society.

EWING, CHEVRON
AND TAMALPAIS

Continuing south along Monterey Bay's shore, the harbor community of Moss Landing lies only a few short miles from the site of the 1912 F–1 stranding at Port Watsonville. Picturesque in its setting along Elkhorn Slough, the tiny bayside community is rich in history and nautical lore.

Over the years a number of mishaps have occurred along the beaches and in the confines of the Moss Landing harbor. Perhaps the most "embarrassing" of all the incidents was the ramming of the Elkhorn Slough bridge by the Coast Guard cutter EWING.

Taking place on October 25, 1961, the EWING had been summoned to the aid of the 50-foot ketch BERUTH which was on fire. Upon entering the harbor and approaching the bridge, Lieutenant Commander Jack Smith, who captained the cutter, reported the crew of his vessel was trying to put the ship into reverse but could not engage the gears. He added that the cutter was traveling at a speed of approximately five knots when she struck the Highway One bridge.

As the 125-foot craft struck the 125-foot bridge, a resounding crash was heard throughout the area, but fortunately there were no injuries to motorists crossing the bridge or to crew members aboard the EWING.

Upon clearing the bridge and inspecting the damage, a jagged gash was found in the bow of the 300-ton cutter, and the 40-ton bridge was found to have been moved approximately one foot out of line! Soon repairs were made to both the EWING and the bridge, and, in ending the tale of this unfortunate incident, it should be mentioned that the undaunted crew of the stricken cutter, with the aid of local firemen, succeeded in putting out the fire aboard the BERUTH.

A second Moss Landing incident that caused numerous heads to turn was the grounding of the 3,149-ton Standard Oil tanker CHEVRON. Fortunately, her cargo of 31,000 barrels of gasoline was not disturbed as the ship became trapped on a sandbar.

According to newspaper accounts of the March 24, 1954 incident, the tanker was "maneuvering toward the dock (in preparation to unloading her cargo) when choppy water and high winds forced her onto a sandbar."

Two company tugs and a Coast Guard cutter are reported to have spent most of the night in attempting to free the tanker from the sand. At approximately 3:00 a.m., with the aid of a high tide, they succeeded in pulling the CHEVRON from the bar. She appeared to have suffered no ill effects from her 10-hour ordeal and proceeded to unload her cargo without further incident.

A second mishap concerning Moss Landing's dreaded sandbars and hidden reefs took place on March 23, 1931, and resulted in the grounding of the steam schooner TAMALPAIS. More frequently referred to as a lumber schooner, the 574-ton vessel was somewhat typical of the coastal freighters that made frequent runs to various Monterey Bay ports. Loaded with 205,000 feet of redwood lumber as she left Moss Landing harbor, the low-riding schooner struck a submerged reef and snapped her rudder. Without a rudder to guide her on her way, the TAMALPAIS was at the mercy of the waves and was soon driven onto the Moss Landing beach.

Captain Adolph Ahlin and his fourteen-man crew were uninjured in the mishap and proceeded to throw much of the lumber overboard in an attempt to free the ship. On March 24th, after most of the lumber had been jettisoned and stacked on the beach (pending transit to its original destination of Santa Cruz), the TAMALPAIS was pulled free of the sand by the tug SEA SCOUT. Upon inspection of the vessel before towing her to a San Francisco drydock, considerable damage to her hull was discovered and special pumps were installed before the craft could make the trip.

After arriving in San Francisco, and after a second inspection of her hull was made, officials of the Little River Redwood Company (for whom the TAMALPAIS sailed) apparently decided she was unworthy of repair, as later in the year the aged wooden schooner was scrapped.

MONTEREY STORMS

Tucked away in the southern corner of Monterey Bay is California's historic first capital city. Long noted for its colorful past, the romantic history of this tourist oriented village by the bay can be found in most volumes of California history.

Perhaps not as well known as her ancient adobes or her picturesque wharfs, but certainly of equal importance from a historic point of view, are accounts of her numerous shipwrecks and her storm-wracked harbor. Discovered in 1602, by the Spanish explorer Sebastian Viscaino, the harbor of Monterey was then described as offering "protection and security" to incoming vessels and to be "very secure against all winds." Perhaps a bit premature in his judgment of the bay, nevertheless it was Viscaino's long-ago discovery and somewhat over-enthusiastic description that set the stage for a colony to be established upon the shores of Alta California.

Even though the bay is listed by most historians as having been discovered in 1602, the actual colonization of Monterey Bay did not begin until 1770. It was in June of this year — over two centuries ago — that the soldier-explorer Gaspar de Portola, and the famed "father" of California's Mission Trail, Padre Junipero Serra, met upon its shores and started a chain of events that made Monterey and its rounded bay the historic hub of Spain's far reaching empire.

From the earliest years it was found that Viscaino's "sheltered harbor" did not live up to his glowing description. Ships frequently felt the wrath of Pacific winds, and waves of immense proportions occasionally pounded the shores of the bay. To this day, even with a breakwater of cement and stone to break the force of incoming waves, ships of various shapes and sizes find their way to the Monterey shore. Records of destructive storms date back to the capital city's beginning years with the "pictured" results of storms taking place in 1915, 1919, 1943, and 1953 (see illustrations), graphically illustrating the scenes of destruction after Pacific storms have unleashed their fury upon the historic harbor of Monterey.

ПАТАLIE

Perhaps the most noted ship to have felt the fury of Monterey Bay winds, and the earliest ship of record to have been lost within the confines of this historic bay, was the schooner NATALIE. With the background of this aged vessel (even to the extent of the spelling of her name) being a subject of considerable controversy, about all one can accurately say of the ship is that if her background is as colorful as the debates that have raged about her, she is certainly worthy of mention.

As the rather involved story goes, the NATALIE is said to have originally been a French sloop-of-war sailing under the name INCONSTANT. It was under this name that the ship is credited with having visited the small Mediterranean island of Elba in the long-ago year of 1815. Of importance to this 1815 port-of-call is the fact that on board the INCONSTANT, as she returned to her homeland, was none other than the exiled Emperor of France, Napoleon Bonaparte!

As Napoleon marched off to meet his Waterloo, the ship that played such a prominent part in his dramatic island escape was seized by rival European powers and eventually became the property of a company with the ambitious plans of colonizing far-off California.

This, very briefly, outlines a portion of the NATALIE's early career and explains how the French vessel found her way half way around the world to the coast of California. While in California waters, additional reports tell of the NATALIE and her alleged activities. Flying the flag of Mexico, she was rigged as a five-masted schooner and served her owners well transporting colonizers from Mexico's Pacific ports to California's coastal cities.

Not long before the NATALIE met her fate on the Monterey beach, she again changed hands, this time to become the property of a group of coastal smugglers. Plying the Pacific under her new command, the NATALIE is reported to have made several successful, although illegal, coastal runs. It was after one of her more profitable trips that the notorious vessel came to her somewhat anticlimactic end.

Moored in Monterey Bay, the NATALIE bobbed peacefully in the quiet waters of California's capital city. Leaving a watch of only a handful of men on board, the captain granted his rowdy band of smugglers a long anticipated night on the town. While celebrating the success of their latest coastal coup, the NATALIE's captain, in the boisterous company of the majority of his crew, joined the local Montereyans at a gay community fiesta — known to early Californians as the Cascarone Ball (celebrated to this day in old Monterey).

With the wine flowing freely and the spirits of the NATALIE's crew swiftly rising to the occasion, a sudden storm swept down upon the peaceful harbor. Involved in more pleasurable pursuits than keeping an eye on the weather, the merry-makers of the Cascarone Ball were completely oblivious to the sudden changing weather conditions.

As the festivities continued into the wee hours of the morning, the gusty north winds outside the ballroom began to raise such a ruckus they could no longer be ignored. Gathering together what members of the crew he could round up, the NATALIE's suddenly sober captain raced toward the beach — only to find his once proud schooner breaking up in the surf!

Reports to this day vary as to the exact cause of the NATALIE's grounding. Generally accepted as fact is the report that the vessel broke her anchor chains at the height of the storm and was blown ashore by the gale force winds. Additional reports state three of the crew members who had remained on board the ship were drowned in their efforts to save the vessel.

As the early morning sun lit up the eastern sky, bleary-eyed members of the NATALIE's crew could be seen salvaging what they could from the storm-wracked ship. Among the salvagers was Montereyan Don Jose Abrego, a Spanish merchant who had been brought to the capital city by the NATALIE when she was transporting colonizers to California's coastal cities. Interested primarily in the timbers of the vessel, Abrego used the prized pieces of hardwood in the construction of his home. (The Casa Abrego is still standing – NATALIE timbers and all – and today is a popular stop along Monterey's Path of History.)

The NATALIE was "officially" identified as the ship that carried Napoleon away from the Isle of Elba by a French Naval officer who visited Monterey and viewed portions of the wrecked ship in 1846. Creating a considerable stir among history minded citizens, a large section of the NATALIE's bow was salvaged and for many years was on display in San Francisco.

Periodically, additional portions of the ship have become exposed as the sands of Monterey beach are constantly shifting. On a September day in 1924, the ancient wreck was again revealed and Montereyan Henry Leppert risked his life salvaging relics of the famed ship. Again, in the late 1920's, reports tell of the aged vessel becoming visible. On this occasion Ernest Doelter and his sons were able to retrieve assorted remnants from the ship such as aged copper and brass bolts, rusted spikes, and a variety of other objects.

Unfortunately for history buffs, a 1971 report printed in the Monterey Peninsula Herald somewhat sank the legend of the NATALIE. The report presented what many consider positive proof that the vessel that broke up on Monterey's beach in the early 1830's was not the same ship that carried Napoleon back to France and his tragic 100-day war. However, positive proof or not, there are many who continue to believe in the history-rich tale – pointing to a number of selected references as their own "proof" that the NATALIE was Napoleon's rescue ship. A partial listing of these sources includes "A History of California," by Alexander Forbes, published in England prior to the 1850's. A second very early reference was an article entitled "Bryon, Nelson and

Napoleon in California," by Alexander S. Taylor, published in 1864 in the respected Pacific Monthly Journal. In 1866 the story again appeared in the book "History of California," by Franklin Tuthill. In following the fascinating story of the NATALIE to the present, there are several post-1900 sources that could be listed, but the majority of these references do little more than repeat previously told tales.

Perhaps it will never be known for sure if Monterey's NATALIE deserves the fame so many have accorded her. . . , but regardless of whether the grand old ship was originally a French sloop-of-war operating in the distant Mediterranean, or served her entire career as a five-masted schooner plying the Pacific, the fact remains a ship by the name of the NATALIE did go ashore on the Monterey beach sometime in the early 1830's. And, perhaps it is of more than passing interest to note, there are those who claim the good ship NATALIE met her own Waterloo a decade — to the day — after the 1821 date Napoleon Bonaparte died (in exile) on the remote Atlantic island of Saint Helena.

The Casa Abrego, built, in part, from timbers of the NATALIE, was constructed in the 1830's and is one of Monterey's oldest landmarks. Located on the corner of Abrego and Webster Streets, the Casa Abrego today is owned by a private women's club. Credit — Randall A. Reinstedt photo.

At one time fitted to carry passengers, the wooden lumber schooner TAMALPAIS is about to be towed from the Moss Landing beach by the tug SEA RANGER. Loaded with lumber destined for Santa Cruz, the TAMALPAIS ran aground on March 31, 1931, after she had lost her rudder to a sandbar upon clearing the Moss Landing harbor. Credit — Allen Knight Maritime Museum.

The storm of April 29, 1915, created considerable havoc along Monterey's waterfront. According to aged newspaper reports, sixty-mile-per-hour winds drove vessels of all shapes and sizes onto the Monterey beach. From the approximate location of where this photograph was taken to the Custom House shoreline, at the far right of the picture, nearly fifty boats were reported to have gone ashore. Credit— Monterey Public Library.

A second view of the Monterey beach after the April 29, 1915 storm. Looking toward the Del Monte Hotel bathhouse pier (which is in the distance and was also damaged by the storm), the damaged "depot wharf" (originally built by the Monterey and Salinas Valley Railroad Company in 1874) can also be seen, as well as the debris-strewn beach and several high and dry boats. Other than damage to numerous fishing vessels, reports state the "northwester" of 1915 did considerable damage to other waterfront facilities. Perhaps of most interest to many local residents was the report that the gale force winds blew the Pacific Steamship Company's office building, complete with a money-filled safe, from the wharf and into the water. Credit — Monterey Public Library.

On Thanksgiving morning, four years after the disastrous storm of 1915, a second scene of harbor devastation greeted the concerned citizens of the Monterey area. With winds blowing from the north, a storm, described as being "the most damaging storm that has ever hit this harbor," struck the waters of Monterey Bay on November 26, 1919. Bringing frustration

With much of the debris cleared away, men of Monterey apply "honest-to-goodness" horsepower in an attempt to pull this victim of the 1919 storm from the beach. In the background a portion of Fisherman's Wharf can be seen, as well as the historic Custom House (the oldest public building on the Pacific Coast — located between the boat and the tree). Pop Ernest's famed restaurant, where the abalone steak was originated, can be seen to the right of the Custom House (two story building with balconies above the stern of the boat). Credit — Monterey County Library.

and despair to people of the waterfront community, the storm did considerable damage to wharves and buildings and claimed a total of 93 vessels that wound up on the beach. Credit — Heidrick photo — Monterey Public Library.

The night of December 8, 1943 brought gale force winds gusting up to 65 miles per hour to Monterey Bay. Described as being the worst storm to have hit the harbor since the 1934 breakwater was completed, the fierce "northeaster" was estimated to have caused losses up to $1,000,000. As dawn broke, a total of 40 boats were counted upon the beach, including three of Monterey's large purse seiners. Credit — Monterey Public Library.

Graphically illustrated in the above two photographs are additional scenes of destruction after the December storm of 1943. Credit — Joe Hinojos photo — Monterey Public Library.

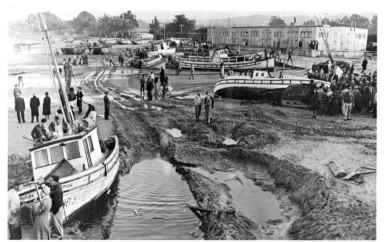

After the tragic "northeaster" of 1943, Fort Ord-based amphibious tanks (as seen in the distance), as well as army supplied tractors and cranes helped clear the beaches and keep losses to a minimum. Credit — Joe Hinojos photo — Monterey Public Library.

The storm of February 23, 1953, brought gale winds of 60 miles per hour to Monterey Bay. Numerous ships, valued at approximately half-a-million dollars, were driven ashore during the storm. The NEW HOPE and the CERRITO BROTHERS, two of Monterey's large purse seiners, were among the victims of the "northeaster," and are shown as they lie together upon the Monterey beach. Credit — Randall A. Reinstedt photo.

WILLIAM H. SMITH
AND AURORA

O ld-time Montereyan Horace Cochran was once the proud owner of two beautiful, but somewhat antiquated, sailing vessels. Anchored in the harbor of Monterey in the early 1930's, the four and five-masted schooners warmed the hearts of many an "old salt" and added a long-lost charm to the historic setting of California's first capital city.

Both of the vessels were brought to the rounded bay in 1932. The five-masted WILLIAM H. SMITH originally hailed from the east coast and was built in Bath, Maine, in 1883. The four-masted AURORA was a product of a west coast shipyard, having been built in Everett, Washington, in 1901. Having served their owners well before calling Monterey their home, the log book of the half-century old WILLIAM H. SMITH showed she had a total of eighteen round-the-world cruises to her credit, as well as many lesser jaunts to numerous foreign ports. While the SMITH was circumventing the globe, the parent company of the AURORA (the Nelson Steamship Company) saw fit to confine the majority of her voyages to the Pacific. Loaded to her beams with California redwood, the gallant four-master spent a good many of her early years in the lumber trade sailing to and from the distant harbors of Australia. She also served many years as a "trader" in the South Seas, and during the First World War she did yeoman's duty as a munitions carrier.

In becoming a part of the Monterey scene, the outdated sailing vessels were rescued from oblivion by Horace Cochran. . . , only to suffer similar fates upon the sands of Del Monte beach. Being the victims of northwest gales, the picturesque schooners met their ends in almost identical ways, at nearly the same location, within two years of each other.

The first to go was the WILLIAM H. SMITH. Being the largest of the two vessels, Cochran had ambitious plans for the five-masted ship and had spent several thousand dollars reconditioning her and building a spacious dance floor aboard her.

Unfortunately for the entire Monterey area, Cochran's elaborate plans for the prized vessel could not be fulfilled. Unable to withstand the northwesterly winds that whipped across the bay on a stormy February afternoon in 1933, the straining SMITH snapped her anchor chain and began her tragic last voyage. A lone watchman, Edwin Berglund, was aboard at the time, but as the SMITH rode with the wind and was at the mercy of the waves, he found it impossible to stop her. Grounding on the beach approximately a quarter of a mile from the old Del Monte Hotel bathhouse, the 1,868-ton vessel dug herself a grave on the white sands of Monterey.

Buffeted by heavy waves throughout the night, the aged schooner began to break up as the new day dawned. By 9:00 a.m. the towering masts could take the pounding no more and crashed to the decks — signaling the end of the WILLIAM H. SMITH's fifty years of wind and sail. People from throughout the Monterey area soon were on hand to comb the sands of Del Monte beach for souvenirs of the picturesque vessel. Owner Horace Cochran himself kept a day-long vigil on the curving shoreline waiting for the SMITH's cabin to come ashore. With the interior of the cabin beautifully finished in Spanish walnut, mahogany, teak, and oak, Cochran claimed the cabin as his own. . . , a fitting memento of a dream that almost came true.

Perhaps not as elegant as the SMITH, but equally as intriguing as an example of the days of sail, the AURORA stood a long lonely vigil in the Monterey harbor after the ill-fated SMITH found her way to the Del Monte beach. Braving the Pacific winds and riding out the stormy waters of Monterey Bay for nearly two years after the SMITH's 1933 grounding, the AURORA eventually followed suit on a January night in 1935. Caught in a northwester, as was the SMITH, the four-masted schooner began dragging her anchor, striking the sands of Del Monte beach at approximately 9:00 p.m. on the night of January 18, 1935.

Grounding stern first, the breakers began an unmerciful pounding of the helpless ship, soon forcing the aged vessel into a broadside position where the full force of the storm-fed waves could do the most damage. By 10:30 p.m., the sands of Del Monte beach were strewn for a quarter of a mile with wreckage from the stranded schooner.

So complete was the destruction during the long stormy night, the AURORA was little more than memories and kindling when the sun's early rays fell upon the white sands of the beach. As with the ill-fated SMITH of two years before, the wreck of the AURORA brought souvenir seekers by the hundreds to the curving shoreline.

Owned by Allen Knight of Carmel at the time of the wreck, plans called for the AURORA to be "beached" upon the sands of Monterey and preserved as a tourist attraction. (Allen Knight, for whom the Monterey Maritime Museum is named, purchased the vessel from Horace Cochran in the summer of 1934.) Enthusiastically backed by the local Chamber of Commerce, the plans were presented to the Monterey City Council at their January 1935 meeting. Interested in the project, but concerned about endorsing the plans without further study, the Council decided to "think it over" until their February meeting.

Unfortunately, while members of the Monterey City Council were "thinking it over," the angry waters of Monterey Bay wrote "finis" to the farsighted plans of providing the historic city of Monterey with a much-needed nautical link to her proud past.

GIPSY

If an award were to be given to the "best known" of the numerous early vessels that visited Monterey Bay, chances are the honor would be bestowed — posthumously of course — on a small coastal freighter known as the GIPSY.

Having operated on the Monterey-San Francisco run (with numerous stops in between) for over fifteen years, the 239-ton vessel kept such a regular schedule she was affectionately called "Old Perpetual Motion" by those who knew her well.

Skippered by a Captain Leland, who is said to have known "every rock and reef" along the coast, the outstanding record of the GIPSY was the envy of ship-owners up and down the entire west coast.

Owned by the Pacific Coast Steamship Company, the gallant little GIPSY plied the coastal waters for nearly three decades and is said to have made more money for her owners than any ship on the Pacific Coast. As an added distinction, it has been rumored that many of San Francisco's wealthiest businessmen started on their roads to success from profits made on the reliable GIPSY.

For a vessel with such a colorful past, the proud little freighter met a somewhat ignoble end on Monterey's Macabee Beach on September 27, 1905. As Captain Leland enjoyed a vacation, the Pacific Coast Steamship Company's relief Captain, Thomas Boyd, skippered the GIPSY as she sailed out of the Golden Gate and made for Monterey Bay. Not as familiar with the coastal markers and buoys as Leland, nevertheless, Boyd brought the GIPSY through heavy seas to a safe anchorage at Moss Landing.

Taking on approximately $15,000 worth of mixed cargo while at her Moss Landing stopover, Captain Boyd soon cleared the port and pointed the bow of the GIPSY toward Monterey. Sighting the buoy off China Point (where Hopkins Marine Station now stands) at 8:00 p.m., Boyd altered his course and made for the shelter of the Monterey harbor. Approximately one mile short of his destination Boyd spotted the fog-shrouded glow of a red light, which he mistakenly took for the marker at the end of the Monterey wharf.

Making for the eerie glow of the light, only a few short minutes passed before a frantic cry from the lookout reported, "Breakers ahead!" Before the reverse thrust of the propeller could take effect, the GIPSY came to a shuddering stop amid the rocks of Macabee Beach. The ship immediately began taking water, and Captain Boyd ordered lanterns tied to her foremast (as a signal of distress) and instructed her whistle to be sounded.

Within minutes the pride of the Pacific Coast Steamship Company listed heavily to starboard, forcing her crew to take to the lifeboats. Fortunately, no lives were lost as the crew made their way to the safety of the beach — only to watch the agony of the GIPSY as she died a slow death amid the rocks and surf.

Unfortunately, the gallant little freighter became a total loss. Additional reports state fishermen, local residents, Presidio soldiers, as well as inhabitants of Monterey's Chinese fishing village, were soon on hand to rescue 400 cases of bottled beer and 100 kegs of steam beer that the ill-fated freighter carried in her hold.

As to the light that was blamed for the ignoble end of the GIPSY, it was nothing more than a red lantern that had been placed as a warning light on a sewer project near the end of Monterey's Hoffman Street.

It is said to this day that no company has ever paid more for a coal oil lantern, as, according to reports, the GIPSY was uninsured. . . , costing her owners approximately $20,000!

The GIPSY wanders no more. For additional GIPSY pictures see pages 68-70. Credit — Hathaway Collection.

Anchored in the harbor of Monterey before her February 23, 1933 grounding, the five-masted schooner WILLIAM H. SMITH added a nostalgic touch of elegance to California's historic first capital city. Credit — Plapp Collection.

With the AURORA in the background, the WILLIAM H. SMITH sits forlornly upon the sands of Monterey beach during the early morning hours of February 24, 1933. Credit — Plapp Collection.

A second view of the WILLIAM H. SMITH taken in the early morning before she began to break up in the surf. Credit — Plapp Collection.

As the day wore on, and as the souvenir seekers and the curious arrived on the scene, the WILLIAM H. SMITH gave in to the sea and broke up in the surf. Credit — Plapp Collection.

The four-masted AURORA as she appeared as a barkentine, long before she became a part of the Monterey scene. Credit – Plapp Collection.

Anchored for a short time inside the Monterey breakwater, the 1,070-ton AURORA dwarfed smaller vessels of Monterey's fishing fleet. Credit – Plapp Collection.

Riding low in the water, the water-logged AURORA is shown anchored in Monterey Bay shortly before her 1935 mishap. Credit — Plapp Collection.

It was less than an hour and a half after her 9:00 p.m. grounding on January 18, 1935, that the AURORA began to break up on the Monterey beach. The above photograph, taken in the early morning hours of January 19th, graphically illustrates what the gale force winds and the angry sea did to the once-picturesque sailing vessel during that long-ago night. Credit — Plapp Collection.

Known as "Old Perpetual Motion," the coastal freighter GIPSY leaves the confines of Monterey Bay in 1901. Credit – Allen Knight Maritime Museum.

The 239-ton GIPSY as she appeared on the rocks after her September 27, 1905 stranding. Credit — Monterey County Library.

Although the date and the location are in error, this rare 1905 photograph clearly shows the broken remains of the once proud GIPSY. Held captive by the Macabee Beach rocks, the stranded coastal freighter became a popular attraction, and numerous people ventured out to the wreck for a personal inspection. Credit — Special Collections, University of California at Santa Cruz.

Said to have made over 1,000 coastal runs without a mishap, the September 27, 1905 wreck sealed forever the fate of the GIPSY. As illustrated in this photo, a large portion of the GIPSY's hull was eventually washed upon the rocks and shore of Macabee Beach. Other than the smartly attired Montereyans inspecting the wrecked vessel, a look at the distant shoreline shows the picturesqueness of the area before Monterey's famed Cannery Row was built. Credit – Hathaway Collection.

FRANK H. BUCK

W ithout a doubt, the most spectacular of all Monterey Bay ship-wrecks was the stranding of the oil tanker FRANK H. BUCK. Opinions differ to this day as to what caused the grounding of this once-proud vessel. Had the wreck taken place during a dense covering of Monterey fog, local citizens, most assuredly, would have nodded in understanding. Or, if a winter storm had turned the Pacific into a night-mare of raging water and gale force winds, perhaps Peninsulans would not have questioned the rather strange circumstances that led to the stranding.

But, reports tell us that at the time of the 9:00 p.m., May 3, 1924, grounding, there was no fog to blot out the powerful beam of the Point Pinos light station, and the Pacific storms had long since departed the northerly waters of Monterey Bay. As a matter of record, reports also state the grounding of the BUCK took place on a clear, calm night.

For these reasons, the question of why the Associated Oil Com-pany tanker wound up high and dry on Pacific Grove's Point Pinos has been debated by residents of the Monterey Bay area for over fifty years. In ruling out fog and rough weather, which have combined to cause the vast majority of shipwrecks along California's 840-mile coast, the ques-tion of human error becomes an important one.

In checking additional records of this long-ago mishap, we find, indeed, that human error was to blame for the near tragic shipwreck. Aged reports tell of the BUCK's Captain Sigmund Anderson setting a course that would have taken his vessel safely into Monterey's rounded bay. After setting his course, Anderson made the mistake of going below deck as third mate George Allen came on watch. Sighting the light of Point Pinos, Allen, who had never been to Monterey, mistakenly ordered a change in the course of the ship and then hurried below to find the captain and get verification of his change. While conferring with the captain, the BUCK struck the rocks at the southerly entrance of Mon-terey Bay.

Traveling at a top speed of thirteen knots, the BUCK slid over two reefs before she came to a shuddering stop, cradled precariously by the jagged rocks of Point Pinos.

A report by the helmsman, who was at the wheel of the ship when she struck the rocks, stated he could clearly see the land, but was not at liberty to do anything about it as he was obligated to obey the orders of his superior. The engine room crew somewhat verified the above report as they stated the signal to stop and go astern was not given until after the ship had struck the rocks.

Members of the crew who had been in their bunks are reported to have raced from their quarters in terror, fearing the ship was in immediate danger of breaking up. One member of the crew who was on deck when the great ship grounded said the towering smokestack shook and rocked as if it were about to collapse.

Having sprung leaks the moment she struck the rocks, the BUCK began taking on water. Fearing the worst was yet to come as the ship showed signs of breaking in the middle, Captain Anderson quickly surveyed the situation and ordered a lifeboat lowered from the seaward side.

Nineteen men, including the ship's second mate, went over the side in the lifeboat. Upon reaching the surf, the men aboard the lifeboat could not loosen the rope that held the small craft to the side of the ship. With waves threatening to capsize the lifeboat, the men worked frantically to free the line. Finally, after several soakings and after being battered against the hull of the BUCK, the troublesome rope broke, enabling the men to row the lifeboat away from the ship.

With the lights of Pacific Grove beckoning to them, the men rowed the lifeboat into the safety of the bay and finally landed at the Associated Oil Company's pier in Monterey.

The remaining lifeboats were rendered useless by the position of the BUCK, as had they been lowered they would have settled on rocks rather than water.

As waves continued to break over portions of the ship, the 408-foot hull trembled from bow to stern. With the fear of her snapping in the middle still uppermost in the minds of the crew, Seaman Adolph Peterson made repeated attempts to throw a line to people on shore who had started to assemble and watch the activity. Finally, as the tide receded and the midnight hour approached, local citizens, led by George H. Pugh, managed to catch one of Peterson's frantic throws. Pulling the line toward the shore they hauled an attached cable from the ship and secured it to a large rock.

With the cable made fast, a breeches buoy was rigged and seven members of the crew were safely transported to shore. Even though these men received a "salty" shower from the breakers as they rode their makeshift carriage to shore, they were happy to be away from the shuddering ship and have their feet firmly planted on dry land.

Carpenter's tools, various pieces of the crew's luggage, and the ship's navigation equipment were also brought to shore with the aid of the breeches buoy.

Fifteen members of the BUCK's crew remained aboard the stricken vessel. Somewhat comforting to these remaining men, although utterly helpless in event of an emergency, was the knowledge that the men of the YALE (who had gallantly answered the BUCK's distress signal), stood by in case they could be of assistance. Also answering the BUCK's S.O.S. was a coastal freighter which had been in the vicinity when the grounding occurred. At 5:45 the following morning a third vessel, the Associated Oil Company's tanker ALDEN ANDERSON, steamed into Monterey Bay with orders from her parent company to stand by until further notice.

Also arriving in the wee hours of the morning (after an all-night auto trip from San Francisco), was George Zay, manager of the Marine Department of the Associated Oil Company. Accompanying him was Captain E. Pillsbury, a representative of Lloyds Underwriters. These two men, in the company of the BUCK's Captain Anderson, set to work immediately and devised a plan they hoped would free the stranded vessel.

While these men planned and the crew members waited, word of the tanker's plight spread rapidly throughout the Peninsula. Not long after sunrise, Point Pinos was alive with people, and a vast assortment of vintage automobiles lined the shore in all directions.

By nightfall the number of people had increased tenfold. Hundreds of pictures had been snapped of the stranded vessel, and artists from nearby Carmel had ventured over the hill and sketched her from every angle. Adding color to the scene were two red-stacked tugboats from San Francisco that steamed into Monterey Bay to be of assistance. Also, the large wrecking tug PEACOCK was soon to enter the picture as she made her way up the California coast from her southerly home harbor of San Pedro.

With plans calling for numerous repairs to be made to the BUCK, and with extensive preparations in order before attempts could be made to refloat the ship, the rescue tugs soon departed the Monterey waters and were replaced by the salvage ship HOMER of the Hanlon Wrecking Company of San Francisco.

Officials of the Associated Oil Company learned from divers that the rocks of Point Pinos had not pierced the oil tanks of the huge tanker (which fortunately had been empty at the time of the stranding), but had done considerable damage to the hull as jagged holes were ripped in the vessel's double bottom.

As the days wore on and patches were placed on the hull of the ship, elaborate preparations for her to be refloated were also being made. Plans called for all repairs and preparations to be completed by the middle of May as the maximum high tides were due at that time.

With the days slowly ticking by, interest in the stranded vessel continued to mount. Visitors from Monterey and adjacent counties continued to line the shore and speculate as to when the mighty vessel would again be seaborne. When L. E. Curtis, consulting engineer for the wrecking company in charge of refloating the BUCK, announced the evening of May 17th as the target date for the first attempt to float the ship, people from far and near made plans to be in attendance and cheer the stricken vessel as she cleared the rocks.

As May 17th approached, the wrecking tug PEACOCK again arrived on the scene and lay at anchor in the company of the HOMER. In anticipation of the maximum high tide, and knowing the great ship might need an extra "lift" to help itself clear the rocks, eight huge hydraulic jacks had been placed under the BUCK's bow (when water under high pressure was forced into the hydraulic jacks, they were capable of relieving the bow of approximately 400 tons pressure). In addition, seven anchors had been planted in the sea two thousand feet from the stern of the ship. Attached to the anchors were cables (each capable of standing a 150-ton pull), which, in turn, were attached to winches on the stern of the ship. The idea behind this rather complicated salvage attempt was that when maximum high tide was reached the hydraulic jacks would give the bow a boost as the winches took in the anchors. Prior to the mid-May high tide, plans also called for air (under high pressure) to be pumped into the ship's 26 empty oil tanks. With the air maintained at a pressure of from five to seven pounds, water would be prevented from entering the tanks if they were to rupture as the ship pulled itself from the rocks.

Additional preparations had also been made to blast the rocks under the bow if it was thought this would aid the ship in freeing itself. Fortunately, dynamite was not needed, as at 8:07, on the night of May 17, 1924, the mighty FRANK H. BUCK — with the aid of a maximum high tide, her eight hydraulic jacks, and the power of her steam winches — pulled herself free of the rocks that had held her a prisoner for a period of two weeks.

As the 6,077-ton vessel inched over the jagged rocks and found its way into the sea (guided by hawsers from the wrecking ships PEA-

COCK and HOMER), thousands of people cheered her triumph, and car horns sent up a ruckus that could be heard throughout the Peninsula.

Riding at anchor in the deep waters of Monterey Bay, a thorough inspection showed the once captive ship capable of withstanding a trip to the harbor of San Francisco. At 4:00 p.m. on May 19th, the BUCK blasted a final farewell to the people of the Monterey Peninsula, and the wrecking tug PEACOCK pulled the tow cable taut and led the crippled tanker toward the Golden Gate. Upon reaching its home port the BUCK was turned over to the Merritt, Chapman, and Scott Wrecking Company, in accordance with its contract to refloat the ship.

For local citizens the exciting two weeks the BUCK graced the rocks of Point Pinos soon became faded memories and little more than a topic of conversation as a Sunday drive was enjoyed around the Peninsula's scenic shoreline. But for the BUCK, its two-week tenure on Pacific Grove's Point of Pines, was but another chapter in an unbelievable tale of a gallant ship that refused to die on a strange shore.

The saga of the FRANK H. BUCK has its beginning in the Bethlehem Shipyards of San Francisco. Launched within days of her sister ship, the LYMAN STEWART (whose launching cradle had rested within fifty feet of the BUCK's), the two identical tankers began their oil carrying careers in 1914. The STEWART was owned by the Union Oil Company and the BUCK sailed for the Associated Oil Company.

With no major problems in their initial years of service, the STEWART and the BUCK proved worthy additions to the fleet of tankers that served their respective owners.

All went well until October 7, 1922. On that fateful day the LYMAN STEWART met its match when it collided with the 8,102-ton steamship WALTER A. LUCKENBACH. Fog was blamed for this Golden Gate mishap, and when the fog finally cleared, the STEWART was observed half submerged, being swept toward the rocks near San Francisco's Point Lobos. Fortunately the entire crew was saved from a watery grave, but the once proud ship was left to die on the rocky shore near San Francisco's world-famed Cliff House.

With the STEWART gone, the BUCK continued transporting oil to various Pacific, South American, and east coast ports. During the First World War the BUCK is reported to have gained considerable notoriety as she was credited with the sinking of an enemy submarine. In 1919 she suffered her first Pacific stranding as she ran aground near San Francisco's Point Montara. Following the Point Montara mishap, the BUCK suffered numerous problems at various other Pacific Coast

75

locations. In October of 1923 she went aground on the Columbia River Bar off Astoria, Oregon. Approximately one month before the Point Pinos stranding she was again in distress. Reporting a disabled propellor off the coast of Eureka, California, she had to be towed to San Francisco for repairs.

Following the touch and go salvage operations at Point Pinos, the BUCK seemed to gain a second life and served the Associated Oil Company faithfully until a dreadful March day in 1937. On that fateful day the BUCK was slowly making its way through the murky fog near the Golden Gate, as was the LYMAN STEWART fifteen years before. Suddenly out of the fog loomed the massive PRESIDENT COOLIDGE, of the American President Lines. A collision was unavoidable and within seconds the COOLIDGE dealt the BUCK a crippling blow.

Taking to lifeboats, the BUCK's crew, as did the STEWART's, were able to avoid a watery grave. Frantic efforts were made to tow the stricken vessel to port, but the BUCK appeared to have a mind of its own and thwarted all attempts to keep it from grounding. Riding with the strong currents of the Golden Gate channel, the BUCK drifted toward the rocks of Point Lobos, soon to break in two upon her jagged shore.

With the BUCK settling on the rocks near San Francisco's Cliff House, she found a final resting place alongside the rusting hulk of her twin sister, the LYMAN STEWART!

Not only did these two vessels die within the shadow of where they had been built, but they met death in the same way, under the same circumstances, in the same area of the treacherous Golden Gate channel, and, possibly most remarkable of all, in death these twin tankers were separated by the exact distance they had been separated in their launching cradles nearly a quarter of a century before!

Credit — Monterey County Library.

Credit — Lewis Josselyn photo — Hathaway Collection.

Photographed from various angles, the stranded FRANK H. BUCK was a must for photographers from throughout central California. Credit—Lewis Josselyn photo—Hathaway Collection.

Vintage automobiles line the shore of Point Pinos as the FRANK H. BUCK remains a captive of the Peninsula rocks. Credit — Monterey County Library.

This dramatic 1924 photograph shows a "dapper" gentleman riding the breeches buoy to the bow of the stranded BUCK. Credit — Monterey County Library.

As spectators make their way across the rocks to get a closer look at the stranded Associated Oil Company tanker, a salvage ship (said to be the HOMER — credited with salvaging many vessels along the central California coast) can be seen in the choppy waters off her bow. Credit — Monterey County Library.

BONITA

As strange as it seems, within a span of twenty-five years, three different vessels by the name of BONITA found their way to the shores of the Monterey Peninsula. Little is known of the steamer BONITA that went on the rocks near Monterey's Coalinga Oil Company wharf on November 15, 1907, except that she was saved by the "timely arrival" of the tugboat DAUNTLESS. And, the 1920 stranding of the relatively small sailing craft BONITA upon the Monterey Beach is hardly worthy of mention, except to state that she was the third BONITA to come to rest upon a Monterey Peninsula shore between the years of 1896 and 1920.

While the 1907 and the 1920 strandings of the above-mentioned vessels are listed because of the coincidence of their identical names, the story of the July 30, 1896 BONITA shipwreck is a tale that should be told, if for no other reason than to report that twelve unfortunate souls lost their lives in this tragic accident.

According to reports of this long-ago mishap, Captain Leland of the 1896 BONITA tragedy, gave the following account upon his arrival in San Francisco:

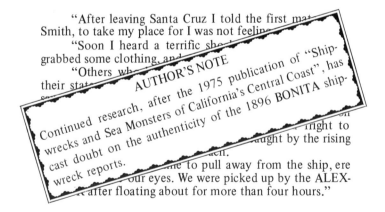

"After leaving Santa Cruz I told the first mate, Smith, to take my place for I was not feeling...

"Soon I heard a terrific sho... grabbed some clothing, an...

"Others wh... their stat...

AUTHOR'S NOTE

Continued research, after the 1975 publication of "Ship-wrecks and Sea Monsters of California's Central Coast", has cast doubt on the authenticity of the 1896 BONITA ship-wreck reports.

...right to ...aught by the rising ...

...e to pull away from the ship, ere ...our eyes. We were picked up by the ALEX-...after floating about for more than four hours."

While Captain Leland's report briefly tells of the events surrounding the tragedy, it does not tell that the "terrific shock" felt by the people aboard the steamer occurred when the aged vessel struck the rocks off Pacific Grove's Point Pinos. Additional information pertaining to the unfortunate shipwreck states that the BONITA was a very old ship and was on her last run when the 8:00 p.m. mishap occurred. She is listed as having sailed under the banner of the Pacific Coast Steamship Company and "was crowded with passengers" on her final run south.

With her death plunge coming approximately one hour after her encounter with the Point Pinos rocks, the BONITA came to rest "in about eight fathoms of water" (48 feet), with the top portions of her two masts remaining visible to those on shore. Being a total loss, pieces of the vessel and portions of her cargo continued to be washed upon the Pacific Grove shoreline for many days.

After their four-hour ordeal of drifting in the darkened waters of Monterey Bay, the BONITA survivors were finally picked up by the top-sail schooner ALEXANDER as they neared the north coast community of Santa Cruz — the last port-of-call on the tragic last voyage of the steamer BONITA.

CG 256

While it is always news when a ship meets its fate on the shores of the Monterey Peninsula, the September 25, 1933, grounding of the 75-foot "rum chaser" CG 256, perhaps commanded more of its share of attention than the average coastal mishap, simply because it was a casualty of the United States Coast Guard.

Home based in San Francisco, the trim steel-gray cutter had been sent to the Monterey area to "observe the sardine strike situation." Being in the Monterey area less than a week when the accident occurred, the CG 256's Captain M. E. Nichol, said of the wreck, "There are no details. We just came ashore in the fog." Fortunately for Captain Nichol and his crew of five, there was only a light sea running when the midnight mishap took place, and all aboard the cutter were able to reach shore safely.

Taking place on the rocks near the north boundary of Moss Beach, the exact location of the accident was directly west of the famed Asilomar Conference Grounds.

Making a routine coastal run when the shipwreck occurred, the CG 256 is reported to have gone ashore "head on," where it lodged between a rocky headland and a group of submerged rocks. Immediately ordering the dual motors of his craft into "full speed astern," Captain Nichol and his crew did all in their power to free their vessel from the rocks. It was not until the cutter's engines became inoperable because of inrushing water, and a jagged hole was found in her hull, that Captain Nichol gave the order to abandon the patrol boat.

When the news of the grounding reached the Coast Guard headquarters in San Francisco, the cutters CG 262 and the McCLELLAN were dispatched to the Monterey area to aid in salvage attempts and to continue the strike duty.

As the seas rose and the news of the shipwreck spread throughout the Peninsula, people swarmed to Moss Beach to view the disabled craft and to watch it being buffeted by the heavy breakers. An afternoon attempt by the men of the CG 262 to put a line aboard the battered vessel ended in near disaster, and as the waves continued to buffet the helpless cutter it became all too evident that the CG 256 was on the verge of becoming a total loss.

By the morning of September 27th, after more than 40 hours of being battered by the relentless Pacific, the CG 256 broke in half. The stern section of the vessel remained a captive of the underwater rocks, but the bow was brought toward the shore by the waves and the incoming tide. As the bow neared the rocky shoreline, Coast Guardsmen from the cutters CG 262 and the McCLELLAN clambered aboard and began salvage operations.

Sending objects ashore on a line, the salvage crew bravely tempted the might of the Pacific as waves repeatedly broke over the bow of the craft, soaking the men and rocking the fore section of the cutter from side to side. Succeeding in saving such items as a light cannon, several rifles, a powerful searchlight, an assortment of instruments, as well as a collection of other valuable articles, the men also succeeded in saving their own lives. . . , receiving numerous salt-water baths in the process.

With salvage operations completed, the men of the CG 262 and the McCLELLAN abandoned what was left of the once trim "rum chaser." (Captain Nichol and the crew of the ill-fated CG 256 had previously been taken to San Francisco by the TINGARD, a third Coast Guard vessel.)

As with the decaying hulk of the RODERICK DHU only a few hundred feet to the south, the cutter CG 256 became a permanent fixture of Moss Beach — a grim reminder of the pitfalls that await an erring navigator.

RODERICK DHU

With her days of wind and sail a thing of the past, the converted oil barge RODERICK DHU came to an ignoble end amidst the rocks and sand of Monterey Peninsula's Moss Beach on April 26, 1909.

Built as a bark, the 1,534-ton vessel was constructed at Sunderland, England, in 1873. Plying the waterways of the world as a full-rigged ship for many years, it was not until relatively late in her career that she was reduced to the inglorious role of transporting oil up and down the Pacific Coast.

It was in this capacity that she met her end along the fog-plagued Monterey Peninsula coast as she was being towed by the tugboat RELIEF. The time was 3:30 a.m., and the tug's Captain Marshall (a veteran of many Monterey runs), mistakenly guided his vessel toward the inlet of Moss Beach thinking he was entering Monterey Bay. Realizing his mistake as the RELIEF neared the breakers, Captain Marshall, with the much needed assistance of his experienced crew, managed to turn the tug around and reach deep water. Unfortunately the RODERICK DHU was not so lucky as she was caught by the heavy breakers and carried onto a ledge of submerged rocks.

None of the crew members aboard the barge were injured as the iron hulled vessel ground to a shuddering stop on the Moss Beach shore. Upon the command of the RODERICK DHU's Captain Haskins, anchors were immediately dropped to keep the ship from being carried farther inland. A line was also passed to the RELIEF, which was kept taut to prevent the ship from swinging upon her anchors at high tide and drift higher onto the beach.

Officials of the Associated Oil Company, for whom the RODERICK DHU sailed, were soon notified of the plight of their stranded vessel. With plans to pull the craft from the ledge of rocks, the tug DEFIANCE was dispatched from her San Francisco port. Arriving at Moss Beach at 3:00 p.m. the following day, the men of the DEFIANCE surveyed the situation and decided to attempt to pull the barge from the rocks as the evening high tide reached its peak.

Working as a team, the men of the tugs RELIEF and DEFIANCE combined their efforts and their horsepower — only to discover that even with the help of the 6:00 p.m. high tide, their efforts only succeeded in listing the crippled ship toward the sea, enabling the heavy breakers to fill her hold.

Discouraged but not defeated, officials of the Associated Oil Company hired a wrecking company out of San Francisco. Upon their arrival at Moss Beach, along with the revenue cutter McCULLOCH (a forerunner of the Coast Guard and manned by a life-saving crew from the Golden Gate station), officials of the wrecking company carefully inspected the stranded ship. As the wrecking company crew surveyed the situation, the men of the McCULLOCH soon realized there was no need for them to remain on the scene as crew members of the RODERICK DHU cheerfully waved to them from the beach. Pointing the bow of their vessel toward San Francisco the McCULLOCH soon departed.

With it all too evident the RODERICK DHU would be in need of extensive repairs (if she were capable of being salvaged), the nine-man crew of the stranded barge, with the exception of the first mate and a lone sailor, were assigned duties in various other Associated Oil Company locations. Meanwhile the first mate and his crew of one set up camp on the sands of Moss Beach where they guarded the stranded barge to prevent looting and unlawful salvage attempts.

After careful inspection of the crippled ship by members of the wrecking crew, officials of the oil company were informed that the RODERICK DHU was beyond salvage. Described as lying on a ledge of rock with a hole stove in her bottom, the wrecking company personnel strongly advised against any attempts to refloat the ship.

Dismayed by the news, oil company officials dismissed the wrecking crew, as well as the crews of the tugs RELIEF and DEFIANCE. Pondering what to do next, the men of Associated decided that perhaps their $175,000 barge was not dead yet. Bringing in divers from the San Francisco area, additional attempts were made to free the vessel from the Moss Beach rocks.

With all attempts failing, and with it becoming more obvious with each passing day that the ship was doomed to remain forever a captive of the Peninsula beach, oil company officials finally admitted defeat and made plans to salvage what little they could.

A hole was laboriously cut through the iron hull of the stranded ship, a steam donkey was dragged over the Moss Beach sand, a boom and block and tackle were rigged above the gaping hole in the side of the vessel, and the process of recovering what was still salvageable was begun. Soon the sands of Moss Beach were dotted with engines, pumps, masts, spars, and rigging. When salvage operations were completed, and when the sands of Moss Beach were cleared, the RODERICK DHU was left to the restless waters of the Pacific.

Having become a popular attraction to Peninsula residents upon her 1909 grounding, the rusting remains of the once elegant ship continued to attract visitors for many years. To this day — nearly three-quarters of a century since her stranding — the salt-eroded remains of the RODERICK DHU can still be seen (during an extreme minus tide) embedded in the rocks and sand of what is now known as Asilomar Beach.

CELIA

Point Joe, where several conflicting currents are said to meet, is clearly visible from Asilomar Beach. Claiming several ships over the years, the restless sea off this rocky promontory is dreaded by mariners up and down the coast.

A 1906 victim of the treacherous waters of this point was the steam schooner CELIA. Outbound from Santa Cruz and heading for Monterey, the 173-ton vessel was loaded with a cargo of lumber when she hit the jagged rocks off Point Joe. Taking to lifeboats when the CELIA's Captain Newman feared his vessel was in danger of breaking up, the crew and passengers of this small coastal freighter spent several harrowing hours in the darkness of the fog-plagued sea before finding their way to Monterey.

Fortunately, no lives were lost in the mishap, but the San Francisco built schooner became a total loss, along with the majority of her 160,000-feet of lumber.

ST. PAUL

A second Point Joe mishap which occurred near the turn of the century was the August 8, 1896, wreck of the steamer ST. PAUL. As with the CELIA, a decade to the month later, the wreck of the ST. PAUL was blamed on a dense coastal fog.

Built in Pennsylvania in 1875, the iron-hulled vessel was sailing for the Pacific Coast Steamship Company when she plowed onto the rocks. Measuring 197 feet in length, 31 feet in beam, and weighing 889-tons, the ST. PAUL was one of the largest coastal freighters to find a final resting place along the shores of the Monterey Peninsula.

Sailing north from San Simeon at the time of the wreck, the ST. PAUL was carrying a cargo of calves and sheep, and was bound for the port city of Monterey. In the vicinity at the time of the 11:15 p.m. mishap, and answering the distress call of the ST. PAUL, was the small coastal freighter GIPSY. Credited with rescuing the ST. PAUL's crew, as well as saving much of the livestock, the gallant little GIPSY, as previously described, met death herself upon a Monterey Peninsula shore in 1905.

Carrying three masts and the figurehead of an eagle, the often-photographed wreck of the ST. PAUL withstood the agony of the pounding Pacific for nearly three months. Then, almost as suddenly as she had struck the rocks, the Philadelphia-built barkentine gave in to the sea, and on a dark October night she broke up and disappeared from view.

The Coast Guard cutter CG 256 as seen before she broke up on the rocks of Moss Beach (Asilomar Beach). A total loss, this September 25, 1933 mishap was blamed on the fog. Credit — Plapp Collection.

Shortly after her April 26, 1909 grounding, the 1,534-ton RODERICK DHU appeared salvageable, and attempts were made to pull her from the rocks and sand of Moss Beach (Asilomar Beach). Credit — Plapp Collection.

Unfortunately, the salvage attempts only succeeded in listing the ship toward the sea, enabling incoming waves to crash upon her decks and fill her hold with water. Credit — Plapp Collection.

With the flag of the stricken RODERICK DHU proudly waving in the breeze, spectators from throughout the Monterey Peninsula arrived at Moss Beach to view the stranded vessel. Sharp-eyed observers will note the United States flag has only forty-seven stars as the Arizona Territory did not become the forty-eighth state until after the 1909 shipwreck. Credit — Plapp Collection.

With the tent of the first mate and his crew of one set up on Moss Beach (to guard against unlawful salvage attempts), and with the future of the RODERICK DHU looking doubtful, members of the vessel's crew await word of their next duty assignment. Credit — Plapp Collection.

With the RODERICK DHU practically on her side, and all attempts to save the vessel forgotten, a hole was cut in the ship's iron hull. With the help of a "steam donkey" (dragged over the Moss Beach sand to the shipwreck site), the process of salvaging items aboard the vessel that were still serviceable was begun. Credit — Hathaway Collection.

As the fog lifted and daylight dawned, the CELIA could be seen from Point Joe. Outbound from Santa Cruz (with a cargo of lumber) and heading for Monterey, the small lumber schooner lost her way and struck the Point Joe rocks on August 28, 1906. Credit – Allen Knight Maritime Museum.

The above photographs show the 173-ton CELIA as she drifted toward the shore and became lodged against Point Joe rocks. Abandoned by her passengers and crew, the CELIA became a total loss. Credit — Monterey County Library

The coastal freighter ST. PAUL crashed upon the Point Joe rocks on August 8, 1896. A victim of fog, the 889-ton vessel became a total loss. Credit — Allen Knight Maritime Museum.

Graphically illustrated in the above two photographs is the constant pounding and buffeting the ST. PAUL was forced to endure before she succumbed to the wrath and fury of the Pacific. Credit — Plapp Collection.

Viewed from still another angle, the ST. PAUL wallowed on the Point Joe shore for nearly three months before she slipped from sight beneath the waves. Credit — Monterey County Library.

With the ST. PAUL in the background, the "squatter's shacks" of an old Chinese fisherman (some sources say Japanese) can be seen in the foreground. Originally called Pyramid Point because of its pyramid-like rock formation (partly visible to the right of the picture), the name of the point was eventually changed to Point Joe, in honor of the squatter who lived there for so many years. Credit — Plapp Collection.

FLAVEL

erhaps not the most spectacular of the Monterey Peninsula's many shipwrecks, nevertheless, the wreck of the lumber schooner FLAVEL generated more "local" excitement than any shipwreck before or after this half-century old mishap.

Outbound from Aberdeen, Washington, and headed for the southern California port of San Pedro, the FLAVEL's decks were piled high with lumber as she groped her way down the fog-shrouded California coast. Suddenly, out of the blackness loomed the rugged rocks of Cypress Point (located slightly south of Point Joe). With nothing anyone could do but "Hold on!", the 967-ton vessel came to a shuddering stop upon the rocky point at a few minutes past midnight on December 14, 1923.

Suffering a jagged hole ripped in her hull, it was soon apparent to all aboard that the ship was doomed to die upon the fog-plagued point. Quick-thinking Captain H. Johnson immediately ordered a distress signal to be sounded from the ship's whistle. Fortunately the signal was heard by H. R. Lyons of Pacific Grove who was on his way home from a late evening dance. Formerly a chief quartermaster in the U. S. Navy, Lyons immediately recognized the signal as one of distress and set out to investigate its source. Upon reaching Cypress Point and realizing the plight of the crew of the FLAVEL, Lyons wasted little time in contacting local authorities. Soon the police, as well as many volunteer rescuers, were on hand to aid in any way they could.

With the ghostly image of the FLAVEL barely visible wallowing in the rough waters of the point, the rescuers on shore attempted to signal the crew of the stricken vessel. For a time dim lights could be seen aboard the ship as members of the crew tried desperately to answer the rescuers' signals. Finally, the flickering of the ship's lights ceased altogether, and no sign of life could be seen aboard the schooner.

With all signs of life gone, the men on shore busied themselves by pacing the beach searching for survivors and huddling around a huge bonfire they had built on the rocks near the point. Talking in hushed tones, the rescuers anxiously waited for the first signs of morning light so a concentrated rescue effort could be made.

As the minutes slowly dragged by, things aboard the schooner went from bad to worse. At approximately 2:30 a.m. Captain Johnson decided it was foolhardy for the entire crew to risk their lives aboard the crippled ship, and ordered his men to board a lifeboat. Following their captain's orders, twenty members of the FLAVEL's crew lowered themselves over the side of their vessel and into the bobbing lifeboat. From the fog-shrouded waters of Cypress Point they rowed their small craft toward the distant lighthouse on Point Pinos.

Upon reaching Point Pinos, the men of the FLAVEL were heartily greeted by Captain Kaichi Takigawa of the abalone boat NORMANDIE, who had been notified of the wreck and had set out from Monterey to attempt a rescue.

After taking the grateful crew to a warm and dry landing at the Monterey wharf, Captain Takigawa and his crew once again braved the fog of Monterey Bay and headed for the stranded schooner to attempt a rescue of Captain Johnson and the two men who had remained with him.

Meanwhile, Captain Johnson had further investigated the condition of his vessel and discovered "her back to be broken both fore and aft." It was 3:30 a.m. when Johnson fully realized the futility of staying aboard the dying ship. He ordered the FLAVEL abandoned and the last of the occupants went over the side. Later, the chief engineer (who had remained aboard with the captain) related how the hull of the ship rolled toward their small craft as if to sink it and prevent their escape. . . , only to suddenly roll back again enabling the lifeboat to right itself and give its occupants a chance to get away.

It was fortunate for Captain Johnson and his two companions that they did make their getaway at 3:30 a.m., as a few minutes after they had abandoned their vessel, she freed herself from her rocky perch and drifted across the face of Cypress Point, finally to again become lodged in the rocks slightly to the north of the point.

Not wanting to risk being dashed against the jagged rocks near the shore, Captain Johnson and his two companions (as did the men of the first lifeboat), rowed their craft toward Point Pinos. Successfully guiding their boat away from Cypress Point, the surprised occupants of the lifeboat were greeted by the men of the NORMANDIE as they neared Seal Rocks (less than a mile from the stranded FLAVEL). Again, Captain Takigawa and his crew groped their way through the fog-blanketed bay and took the weary survivors of the shipwrecked lumber schooner to the Monterey wharf. (It should be noted here that Captain Takigawa and the members of his crew showed extreme courage and exemplified the true camaraderie of the sea as they risked their lives in an effort to rescue fellow seafarers in need.)

While the heroics of Captain Takigawa and his men were taking place, the would-be rescuers on the beach were unaware anyone had left the stranded ship, and they maintained their vigil even as rain began to fall.

Upon receiving word of the wreck, Captain John T. Pierce Jr., of the Monterey Presidio, sent a large truck complete with a squad of men and a spotlight to be of assistance if needed. However, even with the powerful beam of the spotlight, no sign of life could be seen aboard the vessel. Fearing the worst, the band of rescuers counted the minutes until daylight and prayed for the safety of the men aboard the schooner.

It was not until sometime after the sun's early rays began to filter through the fog and rain that the weary rescuers learned of the safety of the crew. With the eerie glow of early morning light clearly showing the outline of the ship, the people on shore shouted and honked car horns in an effort to raise a response from someone aboard the vessel. With no response forthcoming and with the light of day clearly showing the ship to be too far out for them to reach, two of the rescuers made their way to Pebble Beach with a plea to the people of Monterey harbor for a rescue ship to be sent to the aid of the FLAVEL.

It was then they were told of Captain Takigawa's activities of the night before. Taking the news back to their fellow rescuers, the relieved men who had spent the night on the beach were elated over the good news and, after hearty handshakes all around, they wearily went their own ways.

With the crew of the FLAVEL safe on shore, the second chapter of the story of the stranded schooner began to unfold. Boasting over a million feet of valuable lumber lashed to her decks and stacked in her hold (including a vast amount of lumber that had already broken loose and was washing up on nearby beaches), the abandoned FLAVEL represented quite a prize to anyone willing to take the risks of salvaging her cargo.

When the news of the abandoned ship and her valuable cargo began to circulate throughout the Monterey area, knowledgeable parties immediately claimed that — according to the law of the sea — the ship as well as her cargo would become the property of the first person to board her. With this in mind, several concerns, as well as many private individuals, announced their intentions of claiming the wreck.

Four of the interested parties which publicly announced their intent to "battle" for the rights of salvage, as reported in the December 15, 1923, issue of the Monterey Peninsula Herald, were:

1. The Hammond Lumber Company (charterers of the vessel and employers of its captain).
2. The insurance companies that carried the risks on the ship and its cargo.
3. Del Monte Properties Company (owners of the Cypress Point area).
4. A party of local adventurers (led by Paul Flanders of Carmel and James Meehan of Monterey).

With a battle brewing over who had the rights of salvage, as well as a race developing as to who would be the first to board the vessel, people from the entire Monterey Bay area made their way to Cypress Point to watch the outcome of the publicly announced fight.

The first thing that greeted visitors as they arrived at the point was the huge amount of lumber that was already strewn along the shoreline. As to boarding the wallowing schooner, many of the visitors felt it would be foolhardy for anyone to attempt to get close enough to try! Mountainous waves crashed over her decks, and she was constantly being buffeted by the heaviest seas the Monterey area had experienced in many months.

Even with the odds, as well as high seas, against them, the Flanders-Meehan salvaging party left Monterey and made its way toward treacherous Cypress Point. Having chartered an abalone boat for the boarding attempt (complete with small boats, grappling hooks, and other assorted items), the first of the salvage attempts went into high gear.

With hundreds watching, and with luck on their side, three members of the salvaging party (including Paul Flanders) succeeded in boarding the floundering FLAVEL. While on board the ship, Flanders attached a heavy line and sank an anchor with a float on it, stating that he did so in hopes of making his claim to the right of salvage more valid.

On leaving the schooner, Flanders and his mates took compasses, chronometers, side lights, and some cordage. Upon returning to the Monterey wharf, Flanders learned that the other parties interested in salvaging the FLAVEL had joined forces, the outcome being Del Monte Properties Company had purchased the FLAVEL's cargo from the Hammond Lumber Company and, in turn, the right of salvage became theirs.

As for Paul Flanders' claim to the FLAVEL, A. R. Faull (representative of the Hammond Lumber Company), threatened to prefer piracy charges against him for boarding and carrying off the property of the ship. Flanders' answer to Faull's threat seemed to set the matter at rest, as he emphatically stated, "I knew what I was doing before I left Monterey wharf. I'll keep what I took with me!"

With the publicity generated by the fight over salvage, the wreck of the FLAVEL became known throughout the state. On December 16th, two days after the unfortunate mishap, the three-masted schooner played host to over 10,000 people as visitors from throughout central California journeyed to Cypress Point to view the crippled ship. And, it was sometime during that long-ago night that the game schooner succumbed to the greedy Pacific. With her cargo on beaches for miles around, the FLAVEL quietly slipped beneath the restless sea, bringing to a close the dramatic story of the most publicized shipwreck the Monterey Peninsula has ever known.

J.B. STETSON

As has been the case so often with shipwrecks of the Monterey Bay area, fog – the grim, gray, merciless foe of all navigators – was blamed for the grounding of the steam schooner J. B. STETSON.

Treacherous Cypress Point was the location, with the exact site of the grounding being less than one hundred yards from where the lumber schooner FLAVEL struck the rocks eleven years before.

Groping her way through what old-timers state was, "the worst fog they had ever seen," the STETSON came to a lurching, grinding, shuddering stop at approximately 1:00 a.m. on the night of September 3, 1934.

Captain Carl F. W. Hubner immediately ordered Ed Putney, his Chief Engineer, to sound a series of blasts on the ship's whistle. First Officer Sam Christenson took charge of the lifeboats, and Second Officer William Hansen went below to inspect the damaged vessel. Clambering topside, Hansen reported a gaping hole in the ship's hull, excitedly adding, "She's filling faster than the pumps can bail her out!"

With sounds of the crashing surf off the starboard bow, and not being able to see through the fog and darkness of the point, the crew was hesitant to take to the lifeboats. Instead they elected to remain aboard the crippled vessel as it was swept ever closer to the rocky shore by the incoming breakers.

Hearing repeated blasts from the whistle of the stranded schooner, Mrs. J. F. Guthrie, matron of the nearby Cypress Point Golf Club, notified the Monterey Police Department, as well as the night clerk at famed Del Monte Lodge (of the Del Monte Properties Company).

Police officer Charles Scott, upon the advice of Monterey's Assistant Wharfinger James Meehan (of the FLAVEL's Flanders-Meehan salvage party), notified the Coast Guard headquarters in distant San Francisco (there were no Monterey Coast Guard facilities in 1934). In turn, the San Francisco headquarters radioed the cutter DAPHNE, which, by a fortunate coincidence, was in the vicinity of Monterey Bay.

As the DAPHNE slowly began to feel her way toward Cypress Point, Mrs. Guthrie, in the company of her young nephew, walked the short distance from the golf club to the point. Nearing the shore, they were able to hear the distant voices of the crew of the STETSON above the sounds of the pounding breakers, but try as they might they were unable to locate the stranded schooner.

Soon people from Del Monte Lodge, as well as two Deputy Sheriffs, arrived on the scene. Also unable to spot the ship, Harry Hunt, who had driven to the point from the lodge, managed to direct the headlights of his automobile toward the sounds of the crew's voices. With the beams of his headlights knifing through the darkness, the fog-shrouded outline of the STETSON could be seen. Shouting encouragement to the crew, the people ashore let them know the Coast Guard had been alerted and that help was on the way.

Soon Monterey Wharfinger Joseph Alves, along with Meehan and a crew of stevedores, arrived at the point prepared to render aid. But, upon viewing the distressed ship and the pounding surf between it and the rocky shore, they knew it would be foolhardy to attempt a rescue.

As the crew secured themselves as best they could aboard the dying vessel, the two-masted steamer was continually being buffeted by the angry sea. Finally one huge breaker gave the ship a mighty shove, wedging it between two projecting reefs. The cradling arms of the reefs prevented the STETSON from sinking any deeper, but in holding it secure, the crippled schooner was at the mercy of the waves as they broke over her decks, torturing the ruptured hull and shaking the twenty-nine year old vessel from bow to stern.

Having been constructed of wood, the STETSON was no match for the might of the Pacific, and all aboard the craft knew it was only a matter of time before the splintered hull would give in to the never-ending pounding of the waves. Waiting for the first rays of morning light before taking to the lifeboats, or help from the Coast Guard — whichever came first — the crew of the STETSON remained aboard the stranded ship as the crowd on shore continued to grow and to become more alarmed as each hour slipped by.

At approximately 6:00 a.m., to the great relief of all concerned, the Coast Guard cutter DAPHNE majestically appeared through the thick fog. With her powerful lights cutting through the darkness she approached as close to the crippled STETSON as safety would allow. Lowering the lifeboats the thankful crew of the schooner paid their last respects to the dying ship and silently thanked her for "holding on" until help arrived. Braving the breakers, all but three of the twenty-man crew left the STETSON for the safety of the DAPHNE.

Remaining aboard the stranded schooner until the light of morning filtered through the fog were the captain and two of his men. In the dawn's early light Captain Hubner made a thorough inspection of his ship and her water-soaked cargo. With it all too evident that nothing could be done to salvage either the ship or her cargo, Captain Hubner and his two companions bade a sad farewell to the STETSON, and made their way to the waiting DAPHNE.

Heading for Monterey on her fateful last journey, the STETSON was outbound from the southern California port of San Pedro, and was scheduled to pick up 300 tons of merchandise upon her Monterey arrival. Owned by William Gissler Jr., of the Los Angeles Long Beach Dispatch Steamship Line, the trim coastal steamer was valued at $25,000 at the time of her wreck. Battered to pieces by the relentless Pacific, the 837-ton vessel, along with her $5,000 cargo, were soon "chalked-up" as total losses. Only partially insured, the wreck of the STETSON was doubly unfortunate for her owner as three weeks before her tragic encounter with the rocks of Cypress Point she had been completely overhauled in a San Francisco shipyard at a cost of $5,000!

As morning came, so, too, did the people. For additional STETSON pictures see pages 105-107. Credit — Lewis Josselyn photo — Hathaway Collection.

The silhouette of a cypress tree (complete with an impressive assortment of aged automobiles) helps to identify the Monterey Peninsula's Cypress Point. It was here (as seen wallowing in the distance) that the 967-ton FLAVEL's trip from Aberdeen, Washington to San Pedro, California came to an end. Credit — Lewis Josselyn photo — Hathaway Collection.

As the waves continued to buffet her, it was only a matter of time before the floundering FLAVEL became a total loss. Credit — Lewis Josselyn photo — Hathaway Collection.

With her rudder on shore (in the foreground) and a hole ripped in her hull, the FLAVEL begins to give in to the sea. Credit — Monterey County Library.

As high seas continued to pound the helpless FLAVEL, portions of her cargo began to break loose and wash upon the Cypress Point shore. Interested spectators can be seen lining the shoreline as workmen begin the task of salvaging the lumber. Credit — Monterey County Library.

Having sunk from sight two days after her December 14, 1923 mishap, sections of the wrecked FLAVEL, as well as splintered remains of her cargo, continued to wash upon the Cypress Point shores for many days. Credit — Allen Knight Maritime Museum.

A victim of the "worst fog" Montereyans had ever seen, the J. B. STETSON (formerly the CORNELL) became a total loss upon the shores of Cypress Point. Wrecked on September 3, 1934, the 837-ton vessel came to grief within 100 yards of where the FLAVEL went ashore in 1923. Credit — Plapp Collection.

As the fog settles around the J. B. STETSON (upper photo), and the jagged rocks of Cypress Point reach out to sea, the perils that await an erring navigator become all too obvious. Credit — Allen Knight Maritime Museum.

The wooden hull of the J. B. STETSON was no match for the Pacific, and it did not take long for the restless sea to make kindling of the once proud steam schooner. Credit — Allen Knight Maritime Museum.

STAR OF THE WEST

I n leaving the shipwrecks of the Monterey Peninsula, and venturing south, the next promontory that extends into the Pacific is beautiful Point Lobos. Often referred to as "The Greatest Meeting of Land and Water in the World," Punta de los Lobos (Point of the Sea Wolves) boasts a history that is as intriguing as its name. Treasures, pirates, smuggling, whaling, and being the "prize" in a long-ago game of dice, is only part of the history that surrounds this 1839 Mexican land grant.

To add to its colorful collection of tales, in July of 1845 the English brig STAR OF THE WEST came to grief upon this fabled point. Carrying a cargo consisting of such things as casks of liquor, bolts of cloth, and other assorted items of great demand in Alta California, the wreck of the STAR caused great excitement among the population of old Monterey. With nearly half of her cargo put up in "waterproof wrappings" (for purposes of mule-train transportation), the eager salvagers who beat a path to the shipwreck site were handsomely rewarded with choice pieces of frontier finery.

Records do not state how many lives were lost when the STAR OF THE WEST met her fate on the Point Lobos rocks, but records do state that three lives were lost as the over-eager salvagers pitted their strength against the Pacific in their efforts to reap the bounty of the sea. Those who were successful in their quest for "wrecked riches" are reported to have happily led heavily loaded carretas away from Point Lobos and to their homes in nearby Monterey.

In 1900 a relic of the STAR was "rediscovered" in a Point Lobos field. Upon examination the mysterious metal object was found to be the broken bronze ship's bell of the ill-fated British brig. Finding its way to the Peninsula, the antiquated bell became the prized possession of Louis Slevin, noted collector of items of historical significance.

VENTURA AND
LOS ANGELES

B etween the rugged rocks of the Point Lobos promontory and historic lighthouse rock of Point Sur fame, lies what many consider to be the roughest, wildest, and most scenic stretch of coast along the entire 840-mile California shoreline.

Known for its beauty and loved for its ruggedness, the Big Sur coast (as it is known to many) has, over the years, been the graveyard of numerous ships. Two of the better known shipwrecks occurred before the turn of the century. Similar in many ways, the wrecks of the two coastal steamers have frequently been referred to as "twin" shipwrecks. Both vessels were "retired" government ships, both had been renovated for passenger service, both were owned by the Pacific Coast Steamship Company, both mishaps were due to negligence on the part of the ship's officers, both shipwrecks occurred in the vicinity of Point Sur, and both accidents took place in the month of April, within a day of each other, at approximately the same time of night – nineteen years apart!

The first to go was the steamship VENTURA (formerly the USS RESACA). Outbound from San Francisco, the VENTURA was making a run down the California coast, when, on April 20, 1875, at approximately 9:00 p.m., she ripped a jagged hole in her hull on a cluster of rocks slightly to the north of Point Sur (the rocks are estimated to be 300 yards from shore and known to this day as the Ventura Rocks).

According to reports filed after the wreck, the VENTURA's Captain Fake was drunk at the time of the mishap and was in no condition to maintain discipline. With chaos reigning, eleven members of the crew took two of the lifeboats and made their way to shore, leaving the remainder of the crew and the many passengers to fend for themselves. Fortunately, the VENTURA did not immediately sink, and order was eventually restored to the stricken craft, enabling all of the people aboard to reach shore safely.

Met at the beach by early settlers of this remote mountain wilderness, the VENTURA survivors – totaling over one hundred – were given food and shelter by the generous inhabitants of nearby ranches.

A lone horseback rider took the news of the shipwreck to distant Monterey, and it was not long before the steamer SANTA CRUZ was making her way down the rugged coast to pick up the stranded passengers.

As the VENTURA began to go to pieces upon the rocks, much of her cargo was washed ashore. Eagerly awaiting the VENTURA's riches were coastal residents from miles around. Taking what they could carry to their mountain retreats, the plunder of the VENTURA is said to have enhanced the interior of many a coastal dwelling. Other than such items as fine linens and elegant draperies, long ago legends state that a shipment of "knockdown wagons" was also washed upon the Little Sur shore (approximately one mile north of Point Sur). Greatly in demand by the people of the coast, these wagons were prized by their owners, and to this day a number of these century-old wagons are said to still be in use in the backwoods of the Big Sur country.

Nearly a score of years after the VENTURA's April 20, 1875, wreck, the April 21, 1894 wreck of the steamship LOS ANGELES took place (the LOS ANGELES was formerly the revenue cutter WYANDA). Outbound from southern California's Newport Beach and headed for the Golden Gate, the LOS ANGELES carried a crew of 36 and a passenger list numbering 49 — the majority of whom were headed for San Francisco's gala Midwinter Fair.

Unfortunately, those who eventually made it to the Fair were a bit late, and their spirits were somewhat dampened by their harrowing experience at Point Sur. According to reports from Captain Herman Leland, skipper of the ill-fated LOS ANGELES, after the ship had made a routine port-of-call at San Simeon (where 80 tons of wool were brought aboard), he remained on her bridge until they were off Piedras Blancas Point. At that promontory, after having been on deck from 7:30 a.m. to 7:30 p.m., he decided to take a nap and set a "compass course" which would have kept them out of danger until they had passed treacherous Point Sur. Even so, before going to his cabin, he left orders with Third Officer Roger Ryfkogel (who had the deck watch) to rouse him when they reached Cooper's Point (approximately five miles southeast of Point Sur).

As the LOS ANGELES made its way up the coast, hampered by a fierce southwest wind and intermittent rain squalls, Third Officer Ryfkogel failed to recognize Cooper's Point. Having passed the Cooper Point promontory and continuing up the coast, Ryfkogel is reported to have altered the course of the ship, hoping to go inside the kelp beds and gain calmer water.

The altering of the course was subsequently blamed for the shipwreck, as it was the slight change of course that caused the LOS ANGELES to strike a submerged pinnacle of rock approximately 700 yards west of Point Sur. As with the VENTURA nineteen years before, in the confusion that followed, a limited number of the crew contrived to make off with one of the lifeboats. But, unlike the aftermath of the VENTURA wreck, Captain Leland soon had things under control and within less than half an hour all but a few of the eighty-five people aboard the vessel had reached shore safely. Those still aboard were forced to take to the rigging as, thirty minutes after her fateful encounter with the Point Sur rocks, the LOS ANGELES plunged to the bottom of the sea, coming to rest with only the top portions of her masts above water.

Clinging to the masts as they rocked to and fro in the cold Pacific, were Captain Leland and a handful of passengers and crew members. After an agonizing hour of holding on for their lives and praying for help (losing two unfortunate souls in the process), a lifeboat appeared out of the black, and the five remaining survivors were taken ashore.

A final tally showed a total of six people lost their lives as a result of the LOS ANGELES tragedy. The ship was a total loss, and her cargo, consisting of butter, cheese, oranges, lemons, grapefruit, dressed veal, chrome and wool, was strewn up and down the beaches for many miles. The survivors of the 1894 accident were cared for by the warm-hearted people of Big Sur as well as by the dedicated crew of the Point Sur light station. The Point Sur lighthouse had been constructed in 1889 (450 feet above the Pacific on Point Sur rock), and for some unknown reason went unheeded by Third Officer Ryfkogel.

As with the VENTURA, word of the shipwreck was relayed to Monterey by a lone horseback rider from a nearby ranch. Arriving in the early hours of the morning, the rider quickly spread the news of the southcoast disaster. As the word spread throughout the town, numerous people offered their assistance, and soon many people, as well as wagon loads of supplies, were heading down the coast trail.

Welcoming the aid, the shipwreck survivors soon regained their composure and were taken to Monterey by the coastal freighter EUREKA, which arrived in the Point Sur area soon after the accident. Those who didn't relish the idea of a second voyage quite so soon were taken to Monterey in sturdy, safe, and slow lumber wagons (it is ironic that one of the wagons had an accident on the coast trail — precipitating the weary shipwreck survivors into a nearby gulch). Upon arrival in Monterey the subdued survivors of the ill-fated LOS ANGELES were then transported the remainder of the way to San Francisco by rail.

CATANIA

The CATANIA is listed in various sources as having been lost at Point Sur in 1915. While it is true the oil tanker did go on the

Point Sur rocks on October third of that year, it is not true that she became a total loss. As a matter of record, there is a good possibility that the CATANIA's stranding at Point Sur was for a shorter period of time than any other vessel that has suffered the misfortune of ramming the rocks of this central California promontory.

According to 1915 accounts, the CATANIA "went ashore on the rocks off Point Sur and remained fifteen minutes before floating." While fifteen minutes may have seemed like an eternity to her captain and crew, the quarter-hour tenure of her Point Sur stay did little damage to the 3,269-ton vessel and she easily continued on to San Francisco under her own power. Built in 1881, the vessel was owned by the Coast Oil Transport Company, and the cause of her fifteen-minute stranding was blamed on the fog.

BABINDA

L eaving a trail of fire and smoke from the Santa Cruz coast to Point Sur, the story of the last "lonely" voyage of the BABINDA is rather a strange one. Owned by the Ocean Motorship Company, the 3,000-ton vessel was chartered by the Admiral Line and was used extensively in the Pacific Coast freight trade. On a normal coastal run between San Pedro and San Francisco, the BABINDA was struck by fire, "of unknown origin" during the early morning hours of March 3, 1923, while she was off Monterey Bay's north shore. After fighting the raging fire for more than an hour, it became obvious to the BABINDA's captain and crew that it would be impossible to put out the rapidly spreading blaze. Abandoning the vessel and leaving her free to drift, the men of the BABINDA were picked up by the steamer CELILO and taken to San Francisco.

Far from dead, the burning BABINDA rode with the wind and drifted with the current, following a southerly course down the central California coast. Causing considerable alarm as great clouds of smoke continued to billow from her burning hull, the "crewless" BABINDA drifted past the populous Monterey Peninsula, past beautiful Point Lobos, and continued her lonesome last voyage toward distant Point Sur.

Finally, more than twenty-four hours after the crew had abandoned the fire-ravaged freighter, the BABINDA reached the waters of Point Sur. Almost as if she had wanted to join the decaying hulks of numerous other wrecks in this Pacific graveyard, the charred remains of the BABINDA slipped beneath the sea at 7:10 a.m., March 4, 1923. Thus, with the sinking of the gallant coastal freighter, the final chapter of the BABINDA was written. . . , more than a day later, and approximately forty miles from where she had been abandoned by her crew!

hOW ARD OLSON

One of the more recent vessels to have found a final resting place in the vicinity of Point Sur's Pacific graveyard was the lumber schooner HOWARD OLSON. Taking place on May 14, 1956, the 2,477-ton HOWARD OLSON was the victim of a ramming by the 10,000-ton freighter MARINE LEOPARD.

Occurring in the busy shipping lanes off Point Sur, the site of the mishap is reported to have been within two and a half miles of the Point Sur promontory.

With the weather clear and the sea calm at the time of the collision, questions immediately arose as to who, and what, caused the 2:41 a.m. crash. With somewhat different versions of what took place being related by men of the two ships, perhaps it is best to summarize the mishap by saying it was a tragic accident that could have been avoided.

Upon ramming the coastwise steam schooner, the bow of the Luckenbach freighter MARINE LEOPARD sliced through the smaller vessel, cutting it into two separate pieces. The stern section of the 253-foot schooner sank within three minutes, barely giving her crew time to scramble topside and jump into the cold Pacific. The bow of the HOWARD OLSON remained afloat for many hours, finally sinking late in the morning.

Only slightly damaged in the mishap, the MARINE LEOPARD stood by rescuing survivors and notifying the Coast Guard of the accident. The Coast Guard in turn alerted all ships in the area, and sent an amphibious plane and a helicopter from its South San Francisco air station, as well as the cutter ALERT from their Morro Bay facility, and two rescue vessels from its Monterey station. A passing Associated Oil Company tanker, an unidentified tugboat, and the freighter JOHN B. WATERMAN also took part in the rescue. With the combined efforts of all the vessels, and the welcomed assistance of the Coast Guard aircraft, 25 of the HOWARD OLSON's crew were rescued. . . , leaving a total of four men who lost their lives in this 1956 south coast accident.

113

Unfortunately, no photographs are known to exist of the "twin" Point Sur ship-wrecks involving the 1875 wreck of the VENTURA and the 1894 wreck of the LOS ANGELES. Shown above is the steamship LOS ANGELES as she appeared before being lost to the rocks of Point Sur. The photograph was taken at southern California's Redondo Beach pier in September of 1889. Credit — San Francisco Maritime Museum.

The abandoned and burning BABINDA drifted approximately forty miles down the central California coast before sinking off Point Sur. Constructed of wood and used in the Pacific Coast freight trade, the fire-ravaged ship sank on March 4, 1923. Credit — Allen Knight Maritime Museum.

After her collision with the HOWARD OLSON, the 10,000-ton freighter MARINE LEOPARD (of the Luckenbach Steamship Company) remained in the Point Sur area to pick up survivors. Her slightly damaged bow can be seen in this picture, as well as a Coast Guard vessel and helicopter. Credit — Lee Blaisdell photo — Plapp Collection.

115

The bow of the 2,477-ton HOWARD OLSON (of the Oliver J. Olson Company) remained afloat for several hours after her 2:41 a.m., May 14, 1956, Point Sur collision. Credit — Lee Blaisdell photo — Allen Knight Maritime Museum.

Coast Guard facilities can be seen atop Point Sur's Lighthouse Rock. It was in the shipping lanes within sight of Point Sur that the collision between the MARINE LEOPARD and the HOWARD OLSON took place. To the left of Lighthouse Rock the MARINE LEOPARD can be seen as she continues to comb the waters for survivors of the crash. Credit – William L. Morgan photo – Plapp Collection.

Rhine Maru

Slightly south of Point Sur is the mouth of the Big Sur River. Submerged rocks near the entrance to this coastal stream mark the spot where a 6,577-ton Japanese freighter became stranded. Wrecked during a dense fog, the RHINE MARU went aground at approximately 8:00 p.m. on March 28, 1930.

In the area at the time of the wreck was the purse seiner FAIRFAX of Aberdeen, Washington. Captained by H. Merkovich, the FAIRFAX was groping her way through the dense fog when her skipper decided to get his bearings by turning off his engine and listening for the Point Sur foghorn. Instead of the mournful cry of the foghorn, the surprised purse seiner skipper heard blasts from the whistle of the stranded freighter. Cautiously making his way toward the sounds of the whistle, Merkovich soon came upon the grounded ship.

Being buffeted by heavy breakers, the RHINE MARU was listing toward the sea when the FAIRFAX arrived on the scene. With jagged holes ripped in her hull, and taking water in her holds, as well as in her main boiler room, it was clear to the men of the stricken vessel that the ship would remain a captive of the Big Sur rocks for a lengthy period of time. . . , perhaps forever! With this in mind, the crew of the crippled ship wasted little time in lowering her lifeboats and making for the safety of the FAIRFAX when she appeared on the scene.

With all thirty-eight of the RHINE MARU's crew making their way through the pounding surf and clambering aboard the FAIRFAX, Captain Merkovich ferried the grateful men to the combination freighter-passenger vessel HUMBOLDT, which had picked up the RHINE MARU's distress signal and stood by in deeper water. With the transfer complete, and with the Kobe-based crew of the stranded freighter safely aboard the HUMBOLDT, the freighter-passenger liner pointed her bow toward the Golden Gate and steamed away from the fog-plagued waters of Big Sur.

Wasting little time in hiring the San Francisco-based wrecking company of Merritt, Chapman and Scott, the owners of the RHINE MARU had high hopes of salvaging the freighter's cargo, as well as the ship itself. After inspecting the grounded vessel, officials of the wrecking company were optimistic that once the freighter's cargo, consisting of 6,000 bales of double-pressed cotton and 3,000 tons of gypsum, was removed from her holds, she would be light enough to be pulled from the rocks. Once clear of the rocks, plans called for the ship's hull to be patched so she could be towed to a San Francisco drydock.

With the inspection complete and plans set in motion, a crew of fifty men was hired to transfer the freighter's cumbersome cargo to waiting boats. The small boats then took the cotton and gypsum to the schooner PRENTICE, which had been brought to the site by officials of the wrecking company, and which was anchored nearby in deeper water. When filled to capacity, the PRENTICE took her cargo to Monterey and then returned for another load.

The salvage operations were expected to last one month. . . , providing weather conditions permitted continuous work. Unfortunately, the weatherman did not co-operate, and by mid-April, after nearly two-thirds of her cargo had been removed, all efforts to save the stranded freighter had to be abandoned. Lashed by fierce gale winds and assailed by mountainous waves during her stay on the rocks, the $500,000 vessel managed to remain intact until the 13th day of April. But on that unlucky day she gave in to the sea and began to break up in the surf. Standing by, as the 500-foot vessel went to pieces, were the crews of the tugboat PEACOCK and the salvage ship HOMER. Helpless to do anything to save the ship, the men of the PEACOCK and the HOMER considered themselves lucky to have been able to board the freighter and save the salvage equipment that had been secured on her.

Unfortunately, the March 28th stranding of the RHINE MARU not only resulted in the total loss of the ocean-going freighter, but two Monterey-based boats were also lost during the course of salvage. The 46-foot lampara boat PANAMA became a total loss when, on April 9th, she dragged her anchor in heavy seas and was dashed against the Big Sur coast. Engaged in transporting stevedores to and from the stranded freighter, the $10,000 fishing boat was, in a sense, a double loss, as she was only partially insured.

Four days after the PANAMA was driven against the rocky shore, the barge S. CATANIA also became a total loss as she was lost in high seas when she was being towed to Monterey by the salvage ship HOMER.

MAJESTIC

Moving south of the Big Sur River and past Cooper's Point, one comes to Pfeiffer Point, the southernmost promontory covered in "Shipwrecks and Sea Monsters of California's Central Coast". Perhaps not as well known as numerous other points up and down the coast, nevertheless Pfeiffer Point has claimed more than its share of shipwrecks, three of which are covered in this book, and all of which occurred in the early 1900's.

The first of these three south coast mishaps was the December 5, 1909 wreck of the steam schooner MAJESTIC. Returning from Redondo Beach with only 60 tons of ballast as a cargo, the MAJESTIC had the misfortune of running into a raging Pacific storm that brought high winds and heavy seas to the entire central California coast. According to a 1909 newspaper report, "the sea was running mountain high, the rain came down in sheets, and in the darkness one could see but a few yards ahead."

Because of the prevailing conditions, the MAJESTIC's Captain Keegan gave orders to follow a course farther out to sea than usual. Believing he was a full twelve miles off the coast when the MAJESTIC crashed on the Pfeiffer Point shore, the experienced and respected skipper of the schooner could only shake his head in bewilderment and guess that the storm-fed current had carried them toward the shore without anyone on board realizing what was taking place.

Unable to back off the beach, the MAJESTIC became the target for huge waves that crashed against her hull and broke over her decks. Having struck the shore a few minutes past midnight, the men of the MAJESTIC were helpless to do anything about their predicament until nearly 4:00 a.m. Finally, as the storm began to subside, heroic members of the crew succeeded in reaching shore with a lifeline. After the line was made secure, the dazed and somewhat shaken members of the crew who were still aboard the stricken craft, began making their way to shore. It took an additional four hours for the entire twenty-one man crew to reach the safety of a nearby bluff.

Unfamiliar with the Big Sur area, the weary crew of the schooner spent the next four hours struggling up slippery hills and sloshing through rain soaked forests, as they attempted to find a farm or village from which they could get help, and relay the news of the shipwreck to proper authorities.

At about noon, approximately 12 hours after the wreck of their vessel, the MAJESTIC's bedraggled crew reached the farm of John Pfeiffer. Here they were given a most welcome breakfast and a chance to dry their clothing while Captain Keegan made arrangements with Mr. Pfeiffer to be taken to Monterey. Leaving a short time after noon,

Pfeiffer and Keegan followed the storm-wracked coast trail to distant Monterey, finally arriving at 4:00 a.m.

Upon notifying authorities, the revenue cutter McCULLOCH was dispatched to the scene of the stranding. After reaching Pfeiffer Point and examining the grounded vessel, the officers of the McCULLOCH were convinced that nothing could be done to save the ship.

The MAJESTIC's loss was a severe blow to Ira J. Harmon & Company of San Francisco as the lumber schooner was only one year old and her insurance did not fully cover the $140,000 building cost. She was one of the latest of the coastal lumber fleet, and the trim 810-ton vessel had been capable of carrying 1,000,000 feet of lumber.

Pounded to pieces on the Pfeiffer Point shore, the wooden schooner was soon left to the elements as her crew rescued their belongings and were transported to Monterey on two large lumber wagons. Paid off at the Bank of Monterey, the men of the MAJESTIC continued their journey to San Francisco by train.

SHNA-YAK

T he second Pfeiffer Point shipwreck to be described is the July 21, 1916, stranding of the steam schooner SHNA-YAK. The 839-ton vessel was enroute from San Pedro to San Francisco at the time of the mishap and, according to her captain, a dense coastal fog was to blame for the 5:00 p.m. grounding.

Having been without cargo on her trip north, the SHNA-YAK followed the lead of the MAJESTIC and came to grief within 300 feet of where the MAJESTIC had come ashore. Hitting a reef during low tide, the high riding SHNA-YAK didn't appear to be badly damaged until she slipped from the reef and became wedged on nearby rocks, breaking her propeller in the process.

Held fast by the Pfeiffer Point rocks, crew members of the SHNA-YAK took advantage of the low tide and made their way to the nearby shore. Using lifeboats to clear the rocks and reach the beach, all twenty of the SHNA-YAK's crew succeeded in making their way to shore, although the first mate and a fellow seaman were swept away from the shipwreck site, finally to find their way to the northerly shore of Point Sur the following morning.

The men who made it to the Pfeiffer Point beach were met by J. W. Post Jr., who was working at a nearby ranch and heard the distress signal of the stranded ship. Taking the SHNA-YAK's Captain Kose to the Pfeiffer ranch, word of the shipwreck was relayed to Monterey, and arrangements were made to have the crew transported to the distant Peninsula city.

Although the July 23, 1916, Monterey Daily Cypress lists the vessel as a total loss, the SHNA-YAK was not abandoned, and salvage operations were soon begun. It took two months of concentrated work by the Haviside Brothers salvaging firm to refloat the stranded schooner. As the vessel was finally freed from the Pfeiffer Point rocks, cheers from the twenty-five man salvage crew echoed up and down the Big Sur coast. Unfortunately, these cheers soon turned to moans of frustration and disappointment as a high swell caught the schooner as she drifted free of the rocks and carried her ashore again. It took two additional days to once again free the craft, but this time it was for keeps as the SHNA-YAK was immediately towed away from the rock-infested shore and into deeper water.

Having been built at Winslow, Washington, in 1907, the nine-year old vessel survived her two-month stranding in relatively good shape. In 1917, after being refitted in a San Francisco shipyard, the SHNA-YAK changed hands and names — first being called the CHARLES CHRIST-ENSON, and then becoming known as the ANNIE CHRISTENSON. It was by this name she continued to ply the waters of the Pacific Coast, finally to catch fire in 1936 and be scrapped the following year.

Of interest to those familiar with the rugged Big Sur coast is the tale of how members of the salvage crew went to and from the barge on which they lived during their two-month Pfeiffer Point stay. Being anchored near the wreck and just off the rocky shore, the barge proved to be a convenient "hotel" during good weather as a small launch transported the men to and from the wreck, as well as to and from the shore. Unfortunately, good weather and calm water are not always the rule at Pfeiffer Point. When bad weather came, and when rough water separated the barge from the shore, members of the salvage crew desiring to go ashore were forced into taking the tugboat MARIE HAN-LON into Monterey, and then arrange for transportation down the coast trail. This detour took many hours, and when the 96 miles were covered, the men ended up exactly 1,700 feet from where they had started!

THOMAS L. WAND

The third, and last, of the Pfeiffer Point mishaps to be described is the wreck of the steam schooner THOMAS L. WAND.

Coming to rest within 700 feet of where the SHNA-YAK and the MAJESTIC came ashore, the THOMAS L. WAND, like her two predecessors, was not carrying a cargo at the time of her grounding, and was returning from a southern California port.

Blaming the 1:15 a.m., September 16, 1922, wreck on the fog, Captain O. Svendsen of the WAND, stated: "It was the first mate's watch and the thick blanket of fog completely enveloped the ship. The first sign of danger was when the ship struck the rocks midships." Beginning to break up almost immediately, there was only time to give four distress signals from the ship's whistle before the vessel had to be abandoned. Taking to two lifeboats, the fifteen men aboard the ill-fated schooner managed to reach shore safely, even though one of the lifeboats was wrecked in the process.

Lying broadside and pivoting on the rocks as the waves broke over her and spilled from her deckhouse, it soon became apparent that the 657-ton lumber schooner would be a total loss. With her back broken and a hole stove in her bottom, the men of the THOMAS L. WAND, except for her skipper, bade the ship and their captain a sad farewell and left for Monterey on the evening Big Sur Stage. Secure in a makeshift shelter on shore near the ship (which remained a captive of the rocks approximately fifty feet from shore), Captain Svendsen remained with his vessel until the last. With a line attached to the ship, he claimed control of the schooner and prevented scavengers from boarding the craft and taking what they pleased.

In leaving Captain Svendsen on the Pfeiffer Point shore, and in bringing the stories of Pfeiffer Point shipwrecks to a close, it is of interest to note that in attempting to explain the reasons for the numerous shipwrecks along this rugged south coast shore, the September 16, 1922, issue of the Monterey Peninsula Herald carried an article stating, "It is said that there are large quantities of iron ore in the point, and that they cause sufficient deflection of the compass to make navigation difficult when the coastline is hidden in dense fog."

Perhaps there is truth to this long-ago statement, and perhaps it is the combination of fog, heavy seas, strong currents, Pacific storms, and the compass-deviating quantities of iron ore, that caused Pfeiffer Point to become known among long-ago mariners as a "steam schooner's graveyard."

Stranded on submerged rocks near the mouth of the Big Sur River, the March 28, 1930 grounding of the Japanese freighter RHINE MARU resulted in her total loss. Credit — Plapp Collection.

Left to the elements, the lumber schooner MAJESTIC is pounded unmercifully by the Pfeiffer Point breakers. The victim of a December 5, 1909 storm, the one-year old, 810-ton vessel was soon a total loss. Among items rescued by "Big Surites" was the name board of the once trim vessel. Finding its way to the Big Sur country school, it was hung over the door and, according to legend, the school from that time on was known as Majestic School. Credit — San Francisco Maritime Museum.

With pieces scattered up and down the Pfeiffer Point shore, the San Francisco based MAJESTIC was soon reduced to firewood and kindling. Credit — Plapp Collection.

Taken before her July 21, 1916, Pfeiffer Point stranding, the 839-ton SHNA-YAK is shown on a routine coastal run. Credit — Allen Knight Maritime Museum.

After two months of continuous work the SHNA-YAK was freed from the strangle-hold of the Pfeiffer Point shore. After extensive repairs in the Hanlon Shipyard of Oakland (vessel on the right), she returned to Pacific Coast waters under the name ANNIE CHRISTENSON. Credit – Allen Knight Maritime Museum

A September 16, 1922 victim of the fog-plagued waters of the Big Sur coast, the 657-ton THOMAS L. WAND was left to die upon the Pfeiffer Point shore. Credit – Allen Knight Maritime Museum.

MACON

As surprising as it may seem, the most noted shipwreck of the entire central California coast, and of the Big Sur area in particular, did not involve a ship that floated upon water. . . , instead it involved a ship that floated through the air! World-known, and world-mourned, was the tragic 1935 loss of the airship MACON.

Known as the "Monarch of the skies," this gigantic United States Navy dirigible was home based at Moffett Field. Located near the southern tip of San Francisco Bay, Moffett Field still boasts the surprisingly modern-appearing hangar that housed the MACON. The immense size of the hangar (which can be seen from Highway 101) graphically illustrates the size of the elegant silver lady that fit so snugly inside. Being 785 feet long, this "dinosaur of the skies" needed an area approximately the length of three football fields in which to be secured. To further illustrate the size of this long-lost dirigible, if she were to have been placed on end, the grand lady would have equalled the approximate height of a 78-story skyscraper!

The MACON's crew usually numbered between 75 and 100 men, although she was capable of carrying many more. Additional statistics report the MACON to have been powered by eight 12-cylinder, 500-horsepower Maybach reversible motors (which could power the ship forward and backward, as well as up and down). She had a nautical range of over 7,000 miles, and was able to stay aloft for more than 150 hours. She held 6½ million cubic feet of helium gas and traveled at a top speed of 75.6 knots. And, perhaps most spectacular of all, the mighty MACON carried five double-winged Curtiss Sparrowhawk scout planes in her hull!

From this enclosed air-borne hangar, the scout planes were raised and lowered by means of a motorized "trapeze." The planes were also used for defense purposes as the MACON's sole armament was a machine gun mounted in an observation deck on top of its hull — often referred to as "the nest."

Viewed from the ground, the flying aircraft carrier was frequently observed by residents of the Monterey area, and on a gray February morning in 1935, as the pride of the Pacific Fleet headed south to participate in fleet exercises, many local citizens watched the dirigible as it majestically made its way over Monterey Bay and down the rugged California coast. Little did these people know they were watching the historic last flight of the Navy's silver lady.

Upon reaching the area in which the fleet steamed northward, the men of the MACON tracked and plotted the progress of the ships below, and acted as the "eye" of the 34-ship flotilla.

On the afternoon of February 12, 1935, the MACON completed her part of the fleet maneuvers and headed north to her Moffett Field base. Nearing the Point Sur light station at dusk, the airship ran into turbulent weather, and visibility dropped to approximately one mile. Sighting the powerful beam of the Point Sur light through the gloom of the coastal fog, an order was given to steer the great ship away from the shore, as plans called for it to follow the Pacific up the coast in an effort to keep away from the fog-shrouded mountains.

As the order for left rudder was given, reports tell of a strong gust of wind that struck the airship, damaging an already weakened top tailfin. As to what took place next, an account from the master of the light station, who watched the drama from his Point Sur perch, is considered the most accurate eye-witness account that has ever been given. Reporting on February 16, 1935, before a naval board of inquiry (aboard the USS TENNESSEE anchored in San Francisco Bay), lighthouse keeper Thomas Henderson told the following story:

> "I was watching it (the MACON) through glasses. When it was just about abreast of the Point the fin seemed to go to pieces very suddenly. The fabric drifted back. Some of it caught on the rudder.
>
> "I know there was a portion of the frame remaining, but I cannot say whether any of the frame was carried away. The failure appeared to start at the forward end of the fin. The front part rose up, then crumpled back swiftly. I could see a hole at the top of the hull."

With the collapse of the tail fin, the tragic last minutes of the MACON began to unfold. As portions of the top fin tore off, a number of the stern gas cells were ruptured. With helium escaping, the rear of the dirigible began to sink toward the Pacific. In an effort to increase the buoyancy of the craft, an order was given to dump ballast and fuel. Unfortunately, so much was dumped in such a short time the airship rose sharply into the air. In rising to a height of "rarified atmosphere," the gas cells reached an overflow stage and automatic valves were activated, spilling helium into the air. With the loss of the additional helium, the MACON soon lost its buoyancy and began to sink toward the sea.

As it became evident to all aboard that the MACON's end was near, the crew of the great airship prepared for the worst. Orders to don life jackets and to ready life rafts were hurriedly carried out as further orders to abandon ship were awaited. As the MACON neared the sea, reports tell of the choppy waters of the Pacific suddenly becoming calm, as if to provide as peaceful an end as possible for the last of Uncle Sam's super-dirigibles.

Settling into the water stern first, 81 of the 83-man crew managed to gain safety before the massive airship gave up the ghost and sank beneath the waves. Luckily for the 81 survivors, the Navy's 34-ship flotilla was not far away, and within half an hour the cruisers CONCORD and RICHMOND were in the area plucking survivors from the sea.

With the end of the MACON off Monterey's south coast, so ended the history of Uncle Sam's rigid airships — considered by many to have been the most colorful chapter in all of aviation history. To this day, the last of the giant dirigibles rests somewhere beneath the waves off the Big Sur coast (in approximately 250 fathoms of water), and with her in her watery grave lie her five Curtiss Sparrowhawks, and the hopes and dreams of a generation of Americans who believed in Uncle Sam's efforts to prove the value, both militarily and commercially, of the awesome and beautiful monarchs of the skies.

As seen from the front, the mighty MACON is eased into her Moffett Field hangar. Reaching 155 feet in height, 144 feet in width, and 785 feet in length, the MACON certainly deserved her title of "Monarch of the Skies." Credit — Gerald S. Smith Collection — Official United States Navy Photograph.

As dramatic as this photograph is, the immense size of the MACON cannot be truly appreciated until one paces off 785 feet and discovers for himself the true length of this "dinosaur of the skies." Looking at the MACON from the rear, her Moffett Field hangar can be seen in the distance. Credit — Gerald S. Smith collection — Official United States Navy Photograph.

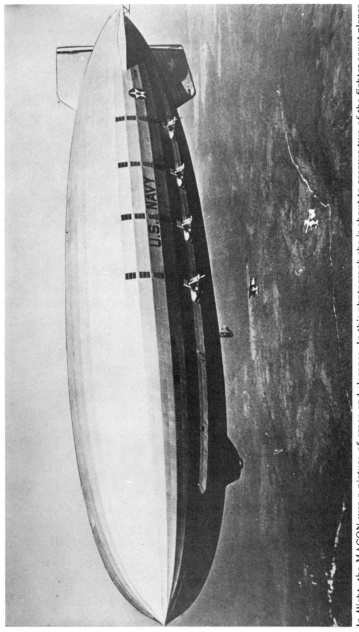

In flight, the MACON was a picture of grace and elegance. In this photograph she is about to recover two of the fighter-scout planes that she carried in her hull. Credit — Prof. Donald M. Layton — Official United States Navy Photograph.

In this dramatic photograph, one of the MACON's Curtiss F9C-1 fighter-scout planes is shown as it makes contact with the motorized trapeze of its mother-ship. Credit — Prof. Donald M. Layton — Official United States Navy Photograph.

In perfect formation, three of the MACON's five fighter-scout planes fly over the MACON's mammoth Moffett Field hangar. Perhaps these are the very same planes that, to this day, rest at the bottom of the Pacific within the hull of the MACON, somewhere off the Big Sur coast. Credit — Gerald S. Smith Collection — Official United States Navy Photograph.

Rifle in hand, a concerned citizen suspiciously eyes the duck-billed head of a mysterious Santa Cruz serpent, while the man to his left attempts to calm a small dog. Below the neck of the serpent can be seen one of the elephant-like legs (complete with ivory toenails) that were reported by a Monterey man to have been in pairs every few yards along the body. For more information and pictures concerning this odd happening of over a half-century ago, see pages 159-165. Credit – Dorothy C. Miller.

SEA MONSTERS

Stories of frightening monsters and snake-like sea serpents have circulated throughout Monterey Bay communities for countless years. Unfortunately, as is the history of most sea serpent sagas, very few pictures have ever been snapped of these elusive creatures of the deep. With the lack of pictures to document the sightings, most tales of Monterey Bay monsters are scoffed at and looked upon as nothing more than nautical nightmares or the figments of someone's overactive imagination.

However, before one scoffs too long and loudly at the multitude of stories and the numerous sightings, one must keep in mind the fact that if there are creatures of the deep that are as yet unknown to man, and if these creatures are prone to venture close to shore (for food or perhaps out of sheer curiosity), the bay of Monterey must be considered an ideal haven for these maritime oddities.

To most people it comes as a surprise to learn that Monterey Bay boasts the deepest underwater trench of the Pacific Coast. Known as the Monterey Submarine Canyon, this great natural abyss has been described by scientists as "one of the world's largest and least studied underwater chasms."

Considering the fact that this "fathomless canyon" extends for many miles into the Pacific, one does not have to stretch his imagination far to conjure up a vast assortment of snake-like serpents and multi-armed monsters that might share Monterey's unique Submarine Canyon and call it their home.

Another favorite hiding place for the monsters of Monterey Bay is said to have been at the mouth of the Salinas River, where a bottomless pit is said to exist! In checking into the stories of the Salinas River pit, and discovering that they have circulated throughout the Monterey Bay area for many generations, one begins to wonder to which Salinas River mouth these stories refer. As most old-time Monterey Bay residents know, the Salinas River's original outlet was through Elkhorn Slough (north of the present-day Salinas River mouth), which meets the sea at the bay-side community of Moss Landing. In following this point of local history one step further, it is of interest to note Monterey's Submarine Canyon is described as being a natural continuation of the Elkhorn Slough-Salinas River channels. With this in mind, one can't help but wonder if the bottomless pit the aged Monterey Bay legend refers to is the very same Monterey Submarine Canyon that more recent stories refer to as harboring a vast assortment of creatures of the deep.

In attempting to describe the multitude of monsters that have become a part of the stories and legends of the Monterey Bay area, one would have to recount numerous tales of multi-humped serpents and snake-like sea beasts. . . , creatures similar in description to various maritime oddities that have become a part of the folklore of many seafaring nations. In discussing these shy creatures of the deep, one must admit the great majority of the tales are nothing more than figments of the imagination or the mistaken identity of such creatures as the enormous blue whale, the grotesque giant squid, the snake-like oarfish, or the evil-appearing octopus. Of course, exaggerated tales, originally told to frighten or impress, are often also accepted as fact by a surprising number of gullible listeners, and soon are being retold as documented accounts.

While the majority of sea monster stories can be grouped into the above categories, one must be careful not to include all the stories in the realms of mistaken identity or fantasized dreams. Perhaps an example or two would suffice to provide proof to the doubters that strange and relatively unknown creatures do exist in the darkness of our ocean depths.

One of the best examples of strange creatures lurking on our ocean floors comes to light in a story that has its beginning in the long-ago year of 1896. As odd as it may seem, the final chapter of this fascinating tale was not recorded until the comparatively recent year of 1971!

The story begins on a St. Augustine, Florida, beach when the remains of a partially decomposed creature of the deep was cast upon the Florida sands. Even though it was studied by numerous people, the identity of the creature remained a mystery until marine biologist A. E. Verrill identified the 12,000-pound beast as a giant octopus. Naming the creature, "Octopus Giganteus Verrill," this granddaddy of all octopuses became the talk of the Florida coast.

Being ten to fifteen times larger than any previously known octopus, Verrill's identification was soon questioned by the astounded public, as well as by his fellow scientists. Finding himself standing alone in his conviction, and finding himself being ridiculed and criticized by other marine biologists, it was not long before Verrill decided that perhaps he had been a bit hasty in his identification, and announced that the decomposed carcass was probably that of a whale instead of an octopus.

This announcement was greeted with much enthusiasm by the questioning public as they now had renewed assurance there were no multi-armed creatures of monstrous proportions lurking on their ocean floors. Soon after Verrill's change of mind the matter was no longer considered newsworthy, and was forgotten.

Three-quarters of a century passed before Verrill's "Octopus Giganteus" again made the news. The year was 1971, and the place was the Smithsonian Institution in Washington, D. C. Marine biologists J. F. Gennaro Jr. and F. G. Wood, with advanced scientific techniques, were able to examine a slice of the creature that had washed up on the Florida beach so many years before. Fortunately, a portion of Verrill's mystery monster had been preserved in alcohol and had been carefully stored at the Smithsonian Institution. With use of a special polarized light source, Gennaro and Wood re-examined the aged creature and found – to the surprise of everyone – that its tissue structure was that of an octopus! If their findings were accurate, and if, in fact, the creature was an octopus, the multi-armed mammoth, when alive, is estimated to have stretched to the unbelievable length of 200 feet – two-thirds the distance of a modern day football field!

While not nearly as startling as Verrill's long-ago find, but much closer to home and perhaps much more believable, is a quote from the 1975 "Guinness Book of Records" which reads: "The largest known octopus is the common Pacific octopus (Octopus apollyon). One specimen trapped in a fisherman's net in Monterey Bay, California, had a radial spread of over 20 feet and scaled 110 lbs." While not boasting a length of 200 feet, nevertheless this Monterey monster was large enough to make the world book of records. . . , and, who is to say there are not octopuses of even larger proportions that lurk to this day in the depths of Monterey Bay?

A nother example of giant creatures beneath the sea, again not as astonishing as Verrill's "Octopus Giganteus," but an example that created quite a stir when it was discovered, was the catch (by a research ship from the country of Denmark) of a giant eel larva. The larva was so large that, by comparison to larva of other species, the mature eel would have reached a length of 90 feet! Since no eels of this size had ever been caught, a second research vessel was dispatched with hopes of capturing a full grown specimen. Probing the ocean depths at the 1,200-foot level, the research vessel managed to "get hold" of something — only to have the unknown creature bend a three-foot iron hook and escape! Scientists to this day are puzzled over just what that "something" was that straightened out the three-foot iron hook.

Going still deeper, we find the previously mentioned giant squid. This evil looking monster of the deep is considered by many to be the most terrifying of all living creatures. Over the years the giant squid has been the basis for numerous sea monster stories, an example of these being the many tales of the multi-armed monster of Norwegian folklore known as the Kraken. With tales of the Kraken dating back hundreds of years, and with the Kraken today generally accepted as having been the giant squid, it is easy to see that monster tales originating from the squid have been with us for a considerable period of time.

In examining the truly gigantic size of the deep-dwelling squid, we find the term "giant" to be very fitting indeed. The largest of these ink-emitting, ten-tentacled creatures that has been recorded, stretched to a huge sixty-six feet in length! Calculated to have weighed a massive 84,000 pounds when alive — one must admit this was a true monster of the deep. In addition to this 42-ton nautical nightmare, there have been unconfirmed reports of giant squid-like creatures stretching to 100 feet in length that have been reported on numerous occasions from various parts of the globe. And. . . , perhaps food for thought. . . , one of the world's acknowledged experts on giant squids, marine biologist Frederick Aldrich (of Newfoundland's St. John's Memorial University) is convinced there are adult giant squids in our vast oceans that are in the 100 to the 150-foot category!

I n dropping from the 1,500-foot depths of the giant squids' domain to a depth exactly twice that deep, we find reports telling of an object of unknown size and shape that has been scientifically recorded. Detected by explosive sonic means, the object, at present, is listed simply as a "sizeable something." With scientific proof that a sizeable object of unknown origin does exist more than half a mile below the surface of the ocean, one must admit there is a distinct possibility that when science finally discovers what the mysterious object is, the world may have positive proof that there are sizeable sea monsters inhabitating the depths of our open oceans.

With a known "sizeable something" at the 3,000-foot level, and with the knowledge that Monterey's own Submarine Canyon drops to over twice that depth near the entrance to the bay — one begins to wonder what, if anything, might also be lurking in the darkened depths of Monterey's rounded bay.

With considerably more than a mile of water between the uncharted bottom of the Monterey trench and the surface water of Monterey Bay, there is certainly more than enough room for various creatures of odd shapes and sizes to live their entire lives, rarely, if ever, being seen. As to just how big this mysterious canyon is, it has been stated by those who know, that Monterey's Submarine Canyon is deep enough to hide the Grand Canyon with a quarter of a mile of "headroom" water to spare!

With a canyon that large only a short distance off Monterey Bay's sloping shoreline, it is little wonder people speculate as to what this submarine world may harbor. Reports of rare and somewhat odd creatures of the deep that have been found in the depths of Monterey Bay have been recorded by various sources over a period of many years. Perhaps the largest documented creature that has officially been sighted in the bay of Monterey is none other than the largest mammal ever to have inhabited the earth — the great blue whale! Inshore visits by these creatures are extremely rare, with scientists attributing their periodic visitations to the Monterey waters to the local submarine canyon. (It is of interest to note, the largest of the blue whales reach a length of 100 feet and weigh in at approximately 300,000 pounds. The whales are so large that an elephant, a man, and the largest known dinosaur could stand on the back of a blue whale and have plenty of room to spare!)

With whales of the 100 to 150-ton category occasionally visiting the waters of Monterey, it must be admitted that Monterey Bay does harbor monstrous creatures of the deep. But. . . , in thinking in terms of sea monsters, the image of a great blue whale does not usually come to mind. Fortunately these peace-loving creatures do not have the killer instinct and, instead of devouring anything that comes within range, they feed almost entirely on plankton (small sea animals and plants). Being the largest and fastest of the whale family, these mammoth monsters also just happen to be toothless!

Several other species of whales frequent the waters of Monterey Bay, including the deadly killer whale. Reaching a length of 30 feet, the killer whales hunt in packs and have been known to gang up on their 100-ton cousins and slaughter them unmercifully. With an abundance of very large and very sharp teeth in their powerful jaws, the killer whale will attack anything that is within reach in its search for food. In the stomach of a relatively small killer whale (14 feet in length), the remains of 13 porpoises and 14 seals were found — quite the opposite of the "dainty diet" his oversized cousin, the great blue whale, is in the habit of eating.

Descriptions of various other whales, sharks, and an assortment of other denizens of the deep could be listed here as residents or visitors to the deep water bay of Monterey (such as the rare sleeper shark that was brought up from the 2,200-foot depths of the Monterey trench in 1974), but in discussing creatures that have been tagged with the term "sea monster," one must be careful not to lump the relatively common inhabitants of the deep, regardless of how large and ferocious they may be, into the monster category. To most people a sea monster is a seldom seen something, usually quite grotesque in appearance that, upon occasion, will rise from the water and scare the daylights out of anyone who has the misfortune of seeing it.

While there are a multitude of sea creatures that might fit within this rather vague definition, Monterey's famed "Old Man of the Sea" perhaps fits better than most. Having been sighted by numerous people over a period of many years, the Old Man of the Sea (the Old Man of Monterey, the Old Man of Monterey Bay, or Bobo the Sea Monster, as it has also been known) has become somewhat of a Monterey Bay legend. While the majority of sightings of this strange creature date back to the heyday of Monterey's famed sardine industry, other reports, both before and after the prosperous years of the sardine, have also been recorded.

Sighted in various parts of the bay, the creature, most often, was reported to have been seen in the early mornings or in the late evenings as dusk settled over the bay. Even though it has been described in various ways by many people over the years, the majority of the sightings follow somewhat of a pattern, as Monterey's Old Man of the Sea was usually described as having a long, thin, snake-like body, and an evil

Labeled as a "freak fish," this Monterey Bay catch of 1907 has puzzled experts for many years. Being somewhat of a mystery to marine biologists, the slender "saucer-eyed" fish has been called a variety of things by a number of different people. With some believing it to have been a member of the oarfish-ribbon fish family, it is interesting to speculate as to how this creature would have looked if it were to have grown to the fifty-foot length of the oarfish. By visualizing the grotesque appearing head approximately ten times larger than it is, attached to a body the length of a telephone pole, one does not have to stretch his imagination far to realize that a creature of such size and appearance could certainly have been referred to as a sea monster! Credit — Special Collections, University of California at Santa Cruz.

This handsome trio represents two unidentified gentlemen and a very dead jew fish. Caught in the Carmel Bay trench in 1908, where fish are said to grow to extra large proportions, the jew fish is an example of the jumbo-sized creatures of the deep that inhabit the submarine canyons of Carmel and Monterey Bays. Credit – Monterey County Library.

Unfortunately, the proud fisherman or details of his catch were not listed on the caption of this long-ago picture. Details that were included described the unhappy looking "critter," with the number 1000 tacked to his side, as a "century-old sunfish," and indicated it had been caught near Santa Cruz in 1940. While the sunfish is not a sea monster, it is certainly not the type of creature one expects to find on the end of his fishing line. Credit — Special Collections, University of California at Santa Cruz.

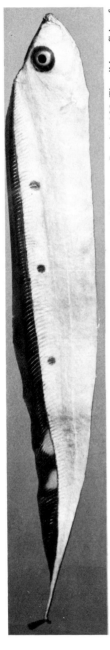

The rare ribbon fish, from which this lifelike cast was made, was caught in the waters of Monterey Bay in 1938. The ribbon fish, of the better-known oarfish family, is known to grow to lengths of over 50 feet. Boasting a reddish crest, or mane, that is said to grow the length of its back, and described as swimming near the surface of the sea carrying a portion of its head above the water, creatures of the oarfish or ribbon fish family have long been referred to as sea monsters. The cast of the Monterey Bay speciman is on display at the Santa Cruz City Museum (Glenn Bradt Junior Museum), 1305 East Cliff Drive, Santa Cruz, California. Credit – Randall A. Reinstedt photo.

Painted in the 1920's by Santa Cruz artist F. B. Tinkle, the significance of this delightful half-century old picture and its original title are unknown. With a portion of the Santa Cruz shoreline recognizable (where a terrified gentleman is about to lose his hat to the snake-like sea serpent), the picture is thought by many to be the artist's rendition of one of the many monster tales that circulated around the Monterey Bay area after the Moore's Beach monster washed upon the Santa Cruz shore in 1925. Credit – Special Collections, University of California at Santa Cruz.

appearing human-like head. The length of the creature has been estimated to have been in the 45 to 150-foot range (although there are
newspaper accounts describing it as being even longer). In discussing
the Old Man of Monterey Bay with several of Monterey's veteran sardine fishermen, they often describe it as having been, "as long as a telephone pole. . . , but much wider." Just how much wider is open to
question. Most old-timers hesitate to estimate the width of the creature simply because all they usually saw of it was its neck and head —
with an occasional glimpse of a hump or two along its slender snake-
like body. The coloring of the body has been described differently by
different individuals, with the majority of opinions agreeing that it was
dark gray in color with irregular whitish spots. The tail of the mysterious Monterey monster has rarely been described, with the most detailed description on record stating: "It was very sharp, tapered, and
had the smallest rudder fins for a body of such size that can be im-
agined. On the underside of the tail there appeared to be vacuum cups
similar to those of octopus tentacles."

In discussing the human-like qualities of the head, one must give
credit to the Monterey fishermen of the 1930's and 40's, as it was they
who most often spotted the creature and in turn vividly described the
head. With animated gestures, many of these very same fishermen will,
to this day, freely talk and tell in detail of their encounters with Monterey's Old Man of the Sea. For doubters of sea monster stories and of
the Old Man of Monterey Bay in particular, it probably would not take
too many discussions with various old-timers of Monterey's famed sardine fleet, to convince them that there is truth to the tales told by these
pioneer fishermen.

Spotted quite frequently over a twenty-year period, the Old Man
of the Sea was a favorite topic of conversation among the crew members
of Monterey's purse seiners (sardine boats). Upon occasion the snake-
like body and human-like head of the mystery monster would be seen
by the entire crew of a twelve-man boat. Telling how the creature
would suddenly surface in the choppy waters of the bay, the dumbfounded fishermen often described the mournful look upon the creature's face and the large, baleful eyes that stared at the ship and the
men aboard. Rising and falling in the water, the long slender neck and
rounded head were at times said to stick out of the water a distance of
eight feet. Even though the mournful look and the baleful eyes were
frequently described, detailed descriptions of the face are hard to come
by as the creature was seldom seen at close range. Grotesque, repulsive,

hideous, homely and terrifying, are all adjectives used in attempting to describe the face of the mystery monster.

Even though many of the Monterey fishermen agree that the face had "hard to explain" human-like qualities to it, there are also those who disagree and, in turn, describe the monster's head in various other ways. Some tell of it being bull-like in appearance (with long, sloping shoulders), while others describe it as being crocodile-like, elephant-like, horse-like, serpent-like and duck-like.

O ther than the human-like descriptions offered by so many of the local fishermen, the crocodile-like descriptions seem to rank second in popularity. For some unknown reason, the majority of crocodile-like sightings were reported by people who observed the creature from shore. In the late 1940's there was a rash of such sightings in the Pacific Grove, Monterey and Fort Ord areas. Almost to a person, the shore sightings tell of the creature being extremely long, approximately four feet in diameter, and multi-humped. Reports of the coloring describe the body as being either tan or gray and the serpent-like head was said to have been flat in appearance with eyes much like those of an African crocodile. The teeth were described as being V-shaped and in an even line, much like the teeth of a saw.

I n jumping from the numerous descriptions of the crocodile-like monster to the creature that resembled an elephant, records indicate both shore parties and fishermen alike reported seeing the strange looking trunk-faced beast. The majority of the sightings took place in the vicinity of the present-day Salinas River mouth and near the entrance to Moss Landing's Elkhorn Slough. For unknown reasons, the elephant-like monster was most often spotted during heavy coverings of Monterey fog. As with the multitude of other Monterey Bay monsters, there are numerous reports of this elephant-like creature. . . , with the following description (credited to an early Monterey fisherman) considered the most detailed of the various accounts that were given: "He had an odd elephant-like trunk that he would inflate and make terrifying noises with. Large reddish eyes protruded from each side of its head which seemed to stare with an evil glow about them. Its snake-like body rose from the water, and small arm-like fins beat at the air as if it was using them to help keep its balance."

As exaggerated as this description may sound, it was told in "sober-seriousness" and the sighting was very real to the individual who saw it. In checking additional elephant-like creature sightings in and around the Monterey Bay, it is remarkable how similar the trunk-faced monster reports are. In attempting to place this red-eyed creature in the realm of reality, local marine biologists were consulted, with the outcome being a somewhat scientific explanation as to what Monterey Bay's elephant-like creature may have been.

According to experts in their field (and backed by numerous books about creatures of the deep), Monterey's mysterious elephant-trunked sea monster was thought to be nothing more than a rare (in the waters of Monterey Bay) elephant seal. In backing up this explanation, the marine biologists described how elephant seals dive to great depths, have an elephant-like trunk, large glowing eyes, and grow to monstrous proportions – often weighing a massive two tons when fully grown!

With these thoughts in mind, and with a "tip of the hat" to our local research scientists, perhaps it is safe to assume that Monterey's elephant-like sea monster was a "misplaced" elephant seal that, for unknown reasons, left the warm waters of southern California and found its way to Monterey Bay.

In carrying the story of the elephant-like sea creature one step further, it can be added that in a 1948 Monterey newspaper account, a respected scientist from Hopkins Marine Station (a branch of Stanford University, located on Monterey Bay's China Point), indicated that he thought the "serpent with an ape-like head" that had been spotted in Monterey waters was a sea elephant with a mussel-like sea animal attached to its face.

Just how or why this could have taken place was not elaborated upon, but if such an event did occur, it is certainly not difficult to imagine what a nightmarish appearing creature the results would have been!

Before leaving the fascinating subject of Monterey's elephant-like sea monster, it should be noted that this evil-eyed creature was spotted with such regularity that it was tagged with the nickname of Bobo – soon to become known as Bobo the Sea Monster. Why the creature was blessed with such an unmonster like name is not known. Perhaps, as many old-timers feel, the name was borrowed from its better known monster cousin of Cape San Martin (approximately sixty miles south of Monterey Bay). Even though these California sea monsters boasted the same name and lived relatively close to each other, they were quite different in appearance. . . , with Bobo of Cape San Martin boasting the face of a giant gorilla! Seen by numerous residents of southern Monterey County, Bobo of Cape San Martin was observed in the 1930's and 40's and was described in numerous publications, including the authoritative sea monster book, "In the Wake of the Sea Serpents" by Bernard Heuvelmans.

I n bringing our discussion back to the bay of Monterey, it should be noted that various features of the multi-faced creature (or creatures) that are said to have inhabited this deep water bay are remarkably similar in a number of ways other than being slender, multi-humped, and elusive. Another rather peculiar characteristic of Monterey's Old Man of the Sea was its most unmonster-like trait of possessing a head topped with flowing red hair (as periodically reported over a period of many years). Again, as with the numerous tales of the snake-like body, crocodile-like eyes, and elephant-like face, the reports of the reddish hair (or long reddish mane) are too numerous to discount.

Scoffers of tales of Monterey's sea monster laughed heartily at the stories of flowing red hair, and wondered aloud what would be added next to the colorful creature. Others, not quite so easily amused, scratched their heads in bewilderment and attempted to attribute the sightings of red hair to seaweed the monster may have adorned itself with, or had been caught in, while surfacing from the depths of the bay. Those who had seen the fiery red hair refused to listen to their jesting and bewildered waterfront friends, and added that the vivid red color of the hair was unlike any seaweed they had ever seen.

In rejecting the jests of the "monster scoffers," and in checking into the stories of Monterey Bay's flaming-haired serpent, a surprising number of supportive facts have come to light. Perhaps most important is the fact that redheaded sea monsters have been reported for as long as man can remember! With confirmed sightings of such creatures from many parts of the globe, there is no reason to doubt that there might also be similar creatures inhabiting the waters of Monterey Bay.

As to what the strange beasts are, scientists from various parts of the world generally agree that the flaming-haired sea serpent is a snake-like fish of the Trachypteridae family, more commonly referred to as the oarfish (also described as the ribbon fish). These seldom-seen creatures are extremely rare and are said to inhabit both the Atlantic and the Pacific oceans. Discussed in numerous publications, the oarfish is said to be gentle, and to be among the strangest of all sea creatures. A quote from the book, "Water Monsters" by Michael Chester, will serve as an introduction to these strange creatures and will also explain the mysterious red hair with which they are adorned:

"A person who reported seeing a creature with all the characteristics of an oarfish might be suspected of having hallucinations. This fish is a very narrow creature — like a ribbon. It measures as much as 40 to 50 feet in length. It is a bluish-silver color, with a flaming red mane. Of course, its mane is not a mane of hair, but is a modified dorsal fin. An oarfish, rippling through the sea, would look like a giant sea serpent.

"Oarfish have rarely been seen, but once in a while one washes ashore on a beach and causes a public sensation. Sometimes oarfish are found with many yards missing from their tail ends. Apparently, large, predatory fish sometimes bite off 15 or 20 feet of an oarfish. But the oarfish seems to live quite well with much of its body gone. In fact, the long tail section of the oarfish and its long mane-like dorsal fin may be its defenses. While a shark or other predator is devouring these trailing, disposable sections, the oarfish gets away."

The book, "Monsters of the Sea" by Barbara Lindsay, also discusses the "ribbonlike oarfish," and tells how one of the famous sea monster legends describes a "sixty-foot sea serpent with a snake-like head and mane on its back." In telling of the oarfish, she goes on to state that the oarfish could easily have been mistaken for such a sea serpent, as it, too, has a mane, "a red crest on the top of its head that stiffens and stands up when the oarfish is alarmed."

Again, in the book, "A History of Fishes" by J. R. Norman, the author relays some interesting information about the seldom-seen oarfish: "The monster described as having the head of a horse with flaming red mane is the oarfish or ribbon fish, a species which probably grows to more than 50 feet in length, and may sometimes be seen swimming with undulating movements at the surface of the sea. The famous Sea Serpent, measuring 56 feet in length, that was cast upon the shore of Orkney (Scotland) in 1808 was almost certainly this fish."

With the preceding quotes all verifying the existence of huge serpent-like creatures with a reddish crest or mane, and with the knowledge that these creatures swim with a snake-like undulating motion — carrying part of their heads above the water (as so stated in "The World Book Encyclopedia"), plus the fact that these creatures are known to exist in the Pacific Ocean, all combine to make one wonder if Monterey's red headed Old Man of the Sea might not have been a giant fish of the oarfish, or ribbon fish variety.

While pondering the plausibility of this interesting possibility, a rather lengthy quote from the files of the Santa Cruz City Museum might help one to arrive at his own conclusion.

As stated in the museum commission minutes (June 5, 1942):

"In the early part of '38 (1938), a rare, deep water fish was caught in our local bay, and turned over as an oddity, to Mr. Turver (the museum director), who had it put on ice. It became a matter of study and speculation to a group of nature lovers, and through them the Smithsonian Institute at Washington got wind of it. The Institute was deeply interested, and wanted it for its collection. Only twice before, had it known of such a catch, and these were comparatively small and mutilated.

"It had been Mr. Turver's intention to make a cast of the fish for our Museum, as the best method of exhibiting it locally. He now replied to the Smithsonian that it could have the fish in exchange for a cast. 'Agreed,' said the Smithsonian. Mr. Turver and Mr. Strohbeen packed it in 105 lbs. of dry ice. Mr. Pendleton carted it over the mountains to catch the east bound train at San Jose. And in early March 1941, it became the coveted possession of Uncle Sam at the Smithsonian.

"Some months later, true to promise, the very carefully-made and beautiful cast, in natural colors even to the sheen of the skin, arrived in Santa Cruz. Since then, out of odd bits of time and as a labor of love, Mr. Turver, in his home shop, made for it a fitting case. Last night Mr. Turver and Mr. Strohbeen put it in position. Today the people of Santa Cruz share with the Smithsonian the distinction of being the only possessors in America, possibly in the world, of a Museum exhibit of a six-foot ribbon fish, drawn from the depths of the sea — in this case, from 600 feet below surface level."

While not "the great white shark" of movie and book fame, nevertheless this basking shark of pre-1900 days looks awesome even in death. Pioneer Montereyans and aged waterfront buildings (with the Custom House to the right and the Pacific Building to the left) add a nostalgic touch to this Monterey scene. For proof that sharks of considerable size still frequent the waters of Monterey Bay, see illustrations on the following two pages. Credit – Monterey History & Art Association.

When Maury Arnold set his net in Monterey Bay on August 6, 1974, he was hopeful of catching fish of the sole or flounder variety — usually measuring from one to two feet in length. Instead, upon pulling in his net, the surprised Monterey fisherman found he had caught the above-pictured basking shark. Estimated to have weighed 5,000 pounds, and reaching a length of over 25 feet, this king-sized "flounder" is another graphic example of the variety of jumbo-sized fish that visit the deep water bay of Monterey. Credit — Ben Lyon photo — Monterey Peninsula Herald.

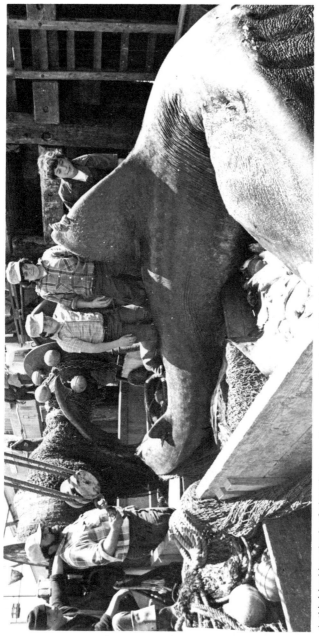

A third basking shark of gigantic proportions graces the deck of the Monterey-based boat DIANA. The shark, measuring 35 feet in length and weighing an estimated 8,000 pounds, became entangled in the nets of Monterey commercial fisherman Joe Pennisi (left) who was fishing for rock cod at the time. Caught near the entrance of Monterey Bay in July of 1977, the shark (as also illustrated in the basking shark pictures on the preceding two pages) proves – beyond doubt – that creatures of staggering proportions are to be found in, and about, the waters of Monterey Bay. Credit – Russ Cain photo – Monterey Peninsula Herald.

Thirteen feet, ten inches in length, and weighing from 1,200 to 1,500 pounds, this female False Killer Whale beached itself upon a Monterey shore on September 1, 1974. While thirteen feet seems rather small when one conjures up the mental image of a whale, the significance of this 1974 event was not the size of the creature, but, instead, the rarity of the happening. According to marine biologists, the all-black mammals make their home in the open sea and seldom come close to land. In continuing their discussion of the beaching, they stated that to the best of their knowledge this was the first such event to have taken place along California's lengthy coast. While not a sea monster, nevertheless this event is certainly worthy of mention as it is another example of rather rare deep-water creatures that are found within the confines of Monterey Bay. Credit — Jim Carmichael photo.

While not a monster 50-feet long, and certainly not caught as it was swimming with a portion of its head above the water, nevertheless the preceding quote serves as proof that the extremely rare ribbon fish does (or did) inhabit the waters of Monterey Bay! On display to this day in the Santa Cruz City Museum, the beautifully prepared six-foot cast also adds considerable credibility to the long-scoffed-at stories of red-headed sea creatures that were once frequently spotted in the local Monterey waters. Also, one must admit, with numerous reports stating that fish of the oarfish-ribbon fish variety, grow to a length approximately ten times the length of the Santa Cruz specimen, the possibility cannot be discounted that at one time there could have been fish in Monterey Bay that boasted flaming red manes, were snake-like in appearance, and grew to monstrous proportions!

Slightly to the south of Monterey Bay lies a second rounded bay. Although not as large nor as historic as its neighbor to the north, nevertheless this second rounded bay is more than comparable in the uniqueness of its submarine canyon. Situated between world-famed Pebble Beach and beautiful Point Lobos, the shoreline of this picturesque bay is praised by visitors for its white sandy beaches, its quaint waterfront homes, and its wind sculptured cypress trees. Known to millions as Carmel Bay, the charm and beauty of this central California inlet has made it a favorite vacation spot for people throughout the world.

As popular as this tourist-oriented bay is, the unique underwater canyon that leads away from one of its many sandy beaches — finally to join the larger Monterey Submarine Canyon — is relatively unknown. And, perhaps even lesser known, is a sea monster "of sorts" that is said to have followed this Carmel Bay canyon to its picturesque shore, where it lolled in the surf for a lengthy spell before turning tail and heading toward the open sea.

Observed by several spectators, this 1948 phenomenon was described quite colorfully in a Monterey newspaper account, as well as in a popular Monterey Peninsula magazine. As stated in the magazine, the monster ventured very close to shore (to the first line of breakers, approximately 40 feet from the beach), where it was minutely studied through binoculars. In continuing with a detailed description of the monster, the article elaborated: "It was shaped like a huge crook-necked squash some forty feet long and about twelve feet wide through the belly section. It was covered with a mottled pelt of grayish green hair studded with barnacles. It had a long, pinkish, wrinkled neck and head. A row of sharp, glassy bottle-green spines stuck up along its back almost two feet high. It seemed to swim by humping itself along like a serpent. It blew spume out of its mouth or head when it surfaced."

Additional descriptions described the tail of the beast as somewhat of a cross between the tail of a whale and that of a shark (vertical in nature), with the pinkish head being compared to both that of a giant snake as well as to the head of a turtle.

The day of the sighting was stormy and the seas were reported to have been running high. However, even with the day being dark and gloomy, numerous well known and respected Monterey Peninsula residents observed the huge beast as it lolled in the surf. Unfortunately, as is usually the case when monsters are sighted, not one of the spectators had a camera with him. Undismayed, a local artist (who was among the awed spectators who viewed the odd beast) took it upon himself (after considerable coaxing by his friends) to paint a picture of the creature as he remembered it. Acknowledged as an accurate likeness by a number of additional witnesses, the picture and descriptions of the beast were presented to marine biologists and co-workers at nearby Hopkins Marine Station. The results of their findings proved to be almost as varied as were the backgrounds of the people who viewed the Carmel Bay creature. With rather vague identifications being given, the end results proved that the creature could have been anything from a bullet-headed whale (which is said to be extinct), to a giant fish of the rare Rhincodon family (the Rhincodon is the largest fish in the world – they are usually found in tropical waters and are reported to reach 60 feet in length).

Perhaps more of interest to Monterey Bay residents, are the thoughts of the late well-known marine biologist Edward F. Ricketts ("Doc" Ricketts is well known to John Steinbeck fans for the part he played in the book "Cannery Row"). Ricketts wondered aloud if the queer Carmel creature could have been an unknown species of pinniped mammal (the pinniped mammal is akin to seals and walruses – identified as aquatic animals with finlike feet or flippers).

Unfortunately the mysterious green-spined, crook-necked creature has never returned to Carmel Bay for further study or positive identification. Perhaps this "forty-foot squash" of Carmel Bay disappeared arm in arm (flipper in flipper) with its Monterey monster cousins to the north — to happily live in the darkened depths of a sub-aqueous world. . . , reminiscing, at times, of its joyful outing one April day along the scenic shoreline of Carmel Bay.

I n describing the elusive monsters of the Monterey Bay area, and in attempting to bring this discussion to a close, perhaps it would be best to describe one monster --- that didn't get away! Traditionally, in the discussions of sea monsters, the end of the tales tell how the monster majestically swam out to sea or mysteriously submerged in a pool of inky black. However, in rare cases there have been reports of strange and monstrous creatures of the deep that have washed onto the world's distant beaches. Two cases in point that have previously been described are Verrill's 200-foot "Octopus Giganteus" and the 56-foot sea serpent that washed upon the Orkney shores over a century and a half ago.

Not to be outdone by beached creatures from other areas, Monterey Bay too boasts a true creature of monstrous proportions, whose carcass was unceremoniously cast upon its rocky north shore. The year was 1925, the place was Moore's Beach (approximately two miles north of Santa Cruz), and the discoverer of the creature was Charles Moore.

Dramatically described in numerous newspapers, the creature soon became the talk of the central coast, with people driving from many California communities to view the strange Santa Cruz serpent. With stories of the creature appearing in so many publications, descriptions of the monster were soon almost as plentiful as the number of people who viewed the odd beast. To give the reader an idea as to how these descriptions varied, and how the monster appeared to different individuals, a selected few of the descriptions are included in this account. The first of the descriptions is from a well known Monterey merchant of a half-century ago. In describing the Santa Cruz beast he told of it being a "serpent-like monster" approximately fifty feet in length, two feet in diameter, with a fish's tail, and a duck's head. Perhaps the strangest feature of all, as described by this Monterey man, were the "elephant-like legs every few yards along the body," and the fact that it boasted a plentiful supply of "ivory toenails!"

A second description, from the Monterey Peninsula Herald, refers to the Santa Cruz monster as a "freak of Father Neptune," and describes it as being thirty-five feet in length, five feet in height, possessing a duck-shaped head, a tail like a whale, and "an odor which kept curious ones at a respectful distance." The newspaper account went on to say geologists, paleontologists, anthropologists, and deep-sea divers were to be asked to "give the creature a close inspection."

According to an account in the Santa Cruz News, the mystery monster was thirty-four feet long, its head was bigger than a barrel, and its eyes were bigger than an abalone. In continuing the report, the newspaper stated it had a great oval shaped body with a neck seven feet long and thirty-six inches in diameter, its body was covered with a coat of "semi-hair and feathers," and its mouth was like that of a duck's bill.

Bernard Heuvelmans, in his authoritative previously-mentioned book, "In the Wake of Sea Serpents", discusses the monster in the following terms, "It was a strange creature, with a huge head longer than a man, tiny eyes and sort of duck's head beak. It was joined to the main body by a slender neck that seemed to be about thirty feet long."

So much for descriptions of the strange beast. As for identifying the monster, numerous knowledgeable (and some not so knowledgeable) men offered their theories, with E. L. Wallace of Santa Cruz (twice president of the Natural History Society of British Columbia) having the following to say about the creature:

> "My examination of the monster was quite thorough. I felt in its mouth and found it had no teeth. Its head is large and its neck fully twenty feet long. The body is weak and the tail is only three feet in length from the end of the backbone. These facts do away with the whale theory (which had been proposed by a handful of other authorities), as the backbone of a whale is far larger than any bone in this animal. Again its tail is too weak for an animal of the deep and does away with that last version.
>
> "With a bill like it possesses, it must have lived on herbage and undoubtedly inhabited a swamp. I would call it a type of plesiosaurus (a plesiosaur was a sea reptile of prehistoric times)."

After continued examination, Mr. Wallace also offered the theory that the monster may have been preserved in a glacier for countless years, finally being released by the gradual melting of the ice, and floating into warmer waters, eventually to be cast upon the Santa Cruz shore.

Another rather interesting observation, which fits into the prehistoric monster category, was offered by the respected Santa Cruz

Judge W. R. Springer. Judge Springer was unsure as to which classification of prehistoric animal the monster belonged, but he felt certain that it was a monster from a past age, "perhaps millions of years old." In describing the creature he spoke of the duck-like head, the twenty-foot long neck, and "evidences of two short feet (or flippers, or fins) beneath the ugly gigantic head."

In continuing, Judge Springer told how the reptile must have swum with its head high above the water, presenting a formidable looking sight to any sailor who may have had the misfortune of viewing it from the watch house.

Finally, in a quote from a Santa Cruz newspaper of 1925, the respected Judge stated, "A monstrosity of the sea would probably best describe the strange creature. Should such a head as it possesses be protruded over the rail of a vessel it would be enough to put the hardest kind of an old tar on the water wagon for life."

With so called "positive" identifications continuing to pour in, the mysterious monster of Moore's Beach was referred to (among other things) as a bottle-neck whale, a bottle-nosed whale, a box-nosed walrus, a shovel-bill shark, and a bottle-nosed porpoise.

While such identifications were being printed in several bay area newspapers, the Santa Cruz Sentinel published an account of a "terrific battle" between a dozen or more sea lions and a monster fish that had been observed (near Santa Cruz's Houghton Beach – a few days before the Moore's Beach monster was discovered) by a Mr. E. J. Lear. As stated by Mr. Lear:

"I was driving a team toward Capitola (a neighboring Santa Cruz community) and suddenly I was attracted by some young sea lions not far out. They were lined up and several large lions were swimming back and forth in front of them. Much farther out I saw the water being churned to foam and thrown high up in the air, and then all of a sudden a big form shot into the air. It was shiny and I took it for a big fish. A dozen or more sea lions were battling it, and every once in a while all would raise out of the water. It looked to me as though all the sea lions were attacking it beneath as the monster came out of the water several times. In telling (of) the battle of that night I estimated its length at 30 feet.

"The battle continued as long as I could see it from the road. I was driving toward Capitola with a load of sand. I have not seen the monster on the beach, but possibly it may have been that which I saw."

With such accounts being printed, and "positive" identifications continuing to be reported by self-proclaimed authorities, it is little wonder local interest in the mystery monster continued to run at fever pitch. Finally, after several noted scientists scratched their heads (and held their noses) over the strange duck-billed beast, officials from the California Academy of Sciences (who officially claimed the body of the mammal for scientific study) carefully inspected the creature's skull, and announced to the waiting world that the mysterious monster of Moore's Beach was a North Pacific type of beaked whale. This creature was described as being so rare that no name, except its Latin one, Berardius bairdi (given to it by Leonhard Stejneger in 1883), had ever been bestowed upon it!

With the mystery monster "officially" tagged with a name, and with further reports stating such things as the dual effects of decomposition and high seas had separated the body from the skin, which in turn had rolled up on itself to create the illusion of a long neck, all seemingly to fall into place, most bay area residents nodded in agreement and readily accepted the Academy's findings — soon to forget the entire episode. But, regardless of the number of people who accepted the Academy's findings, there were also those who refused to believe the creature was a member of the whale family, and steadfastly clung to the belief that the Moore's Beach monster was of unknown origin. . . , perhaps a throwback to prehistoric times.

Of interest at this point is the information that these events of over half a century ago predate the 1938 discovery of a "prehistoric" coelacanth by thirteen years! The coelacanth is a species of fish that lived so long ago, and was so rare it had officially been labeled as extinct. So extinct was this fish that scientists listed it as having died out approximately 70 million years ago! With the 1938 catch of a fish of this type, it was proven, beyond doubt, that creatures of prehistoric times do exist to this day in our underwater world.

With this thought in mind, combined with the fact that so little is known of Monterey's Submarine Canyon (not to mention the number of rare and record-making catches that have already been taken from the waters of this bay), one must admit it would be most unwise to be hasty in his judgement of what does or does not exist in the uncharted canyons of this central California harbor.

Whether the Moore's Beach monster of Santa Cruz was or was not a rare beaked whale of North Pacific waters may not be the question. Perhaps instead we should ask, is it possible that creatures as yet unknown to man could exist in the depths of Monterey Bay? If the answer to this question is yes. . . , perhaps we should also ask if Bobo the Sea Monster, the Old Man of the Sea, the flaming haired sea serpent, as well as numerous other unidentified creatures that have been sighted in Monterey waters over the years, could have been true monsters of the deep — rather than figments of the imagination or nautical fantasies fashioned by glory-seeking fishermen?

The answers to these questions must remain with the reader. The facts have been presented as accurately as possible, and the questions have been asked. It is now up to the reader to decide for himself whether or not there are (or have ever been) sea monsters "of sorts" in California's Monterey Bay.

The rocky shelf of Moore's Beach and the Santa Cruz sea monster as seen from a nearby cliff. Perhaps it was from this exact spot that Charles Moore spotted the grotesque remains of the sea beast over half a century ago. Credit — Special Collections, University of California at Santa Cruz.

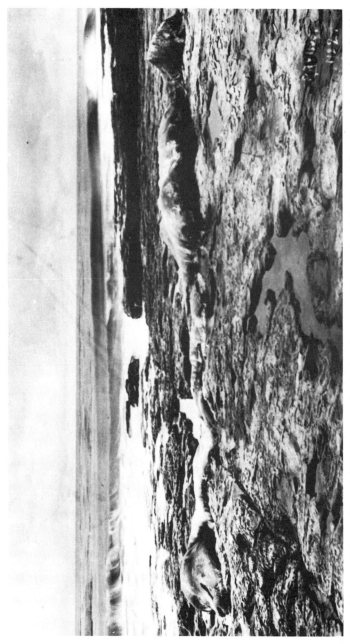

Viewed from a distance, it is not difficult to see why the lengthy serpent-like remains of the Moore's Beach monster was described in such a variety of ways by different individuals. Credit — Special Collections, University of California at Santa Cruz.

Long dead, the Santa Cruz serpent, or rare beaked whale, possessed what appeared to be a long narrow neck, with the bulk of the body connected at the rear. A group of north coast young men and an avid photographer and his dedicated spouse can also be seen in this aged photo. Credit — Special Collections, University of California at Santa Cruz.

A second Moore's Beach monster of massive proportions drew a crowd of elegantly attired spectators when it washed upon the Santa Cruz shore approximately three-quarters of a century ago. Identified as a blue whale, the creature stretched to an estimated 50 feet in length. Credit — Wilder Ranch State Park.

As indicated in the text, even though whales must be considered monsters of the deep, they are not what one thinks of when the subject of sea monsters comes to mind. Nevertheless, it should be noted that Monterey of old was a whaling port, and over the years many monstrous mammals of the whale variety were caught in and around the waters of Monterey Bay. As the years progressed, Monterey's neighbors to the north (Moss Landing — Monterey Bay) and the south (Whaler's Cove — Carmel Bay) took up the cry of "Thar she blows!", and became whaling ports in their own rights. Taken at Moss Landing in the early 1900s, the picture at right shows a nattily dressed young man posing between the gaping jaws of a sperm whale. Although not considered a sea monster (at least of the scary variety), one must admit that the photograph proves — in a most graphic way — that whales are certainly monsters when it comes to size! Credit — L.S. Slevin photo — Hathaway Collection.

167

SUMMARY

In summation, it is sincerely hoped by the author that "Shipwrecks and Sea Monsters of California's Central Coast" has brought enjoyment to the reader and has helped the reader become more aware of the maritime memories and the nautical lore that has played such an important part in making California's beautiful central coast the unique and historically rich area that it is.